THE NEXT STEP

BABYWISE

Gary Ezzo & Robert Bucknam, M.D.

GROWING FAMILIES
INTERNATIONAL

BABYWISE II
Parenting Your Pretoddler
(5-15 Months)

Copyright 1994 by Growing Families International

Published by Growing Families International Press, Chatsworth, California 91311

Printed in the United States of America

ISBN:1-883035-98-8

Dedicated to

Ashley and Whitney

Acknowledgements

We are grateful for the assistance given us by many co-workers, including Tim and Patricia Lentz, Scott and Theresa McLeod, David and Cynthia Iglesias, Tiana Wendelburg, and Sharon Augustson, all who contributed to the preparation of this text.

We are also grateful to Connie Lamoureux for her contribution on language development (*Appendix A*) and Nancy Martin and sketch artist Yvonne Wilber for their contribution on sign language training (*Appendix B*).

Finally a special thanks to our friends and teaching colleagues: Eric and Julie Abel, and Gary and Robyn Vander Weide. Their collective wisdom and applied experience gives this series its practical disposition.

Foreword, Introduction, and Chapter Divisions

Foreword

As a pediatrician, I am concerned about healthy children. Healthy means more than just positive ear, nose, and throat examinations. Healthy growth includes physical, moral, and academic fitness. *BABYWISE II* touches on each of these categories.

Parenting a pretoddler arouses many different emotions. The emotions of love, joy, peace, contentment, and confidence are easily matched by the emotions of frustration, disappointment, and discouragement, (and on some days, despair). Parenting to achieve all the right emotions is not the genesis of child training. Yet many parents believe exactly that. For them, childrearing is reduced to avoidance of all the negative emotions and pursuit of all the positive ones. Thus right and wrong training is measured by how parents think their child feels rather then by the end product——their child's behavior. Feelings belonging to both parent and child become the basis of nurturing. If the child feels happy, the parent is satisfied. If the child feels sad, then the parent works to create an environment that will eliminate his sadness. That approach is not healthy for children, families, or society at large.

The ultimate objective of parenting in a free society is a moral one. The duty of every parent is to raise a morally responsible child who will grow up to be a morally responsible adult. Such an important task should not be put off to the later years. The job of every parent is to raise a child who at each phase of growth is a blessing not only to them, but to everyone else around.

We base this book on a moral model of child development, not a psychological one. By that we mean moral training (yes, even in the pretoddler phase), is the genesis of child-rearing. The result being a healthy, happy, and relationally secure life.

Moral training is a priority discipline. The success achieved in all the major disciplines of life (i.e., skills development, academic achievement, and interpersonal relationships), is tied to and dependent on the quality of moral training. Children who have internal self-control and mastery in the please and thank you's of life also have the self-control that secures for them a healthy academic and relational life. The moral self-control that keeps a child sitting in a high chair without fighting with Mom is the same self-control that will keep him at a desk with a book in his hand. The battle for right high chair manners is moral, not academic. In fact, most of what parents do by way of training in the early months and years serves a broader moral purpose.

Why then is moral training important? When you rightly train the heart of a child, you lay down a right foundation for the other disciplines of life. And the results show. Parents tell me that not only are they wonderfully pleased with the results of this second series, but their friends and relatives stand in amazement of the accomplishments of their pretoddler. *BABYWISE* laid down the right foundation; *BABYWISE II* provides the right structure that creates a suitable learning environment that will advance any child in the needed disciplines of life.

To experience the right emotions in parenting, right training is a prerequisite. *BABYWISE II* will help advance that cause.

Robert Bucknam, M.D.
Louisville, CO

Introduction

Reality! You are at least five months into your tour of parenting. The complexity of child training now starts to come into focus. As your baby matures, both constant and variable factors continually influence his development. As he moves into the pretoddler phase, the variables of growth begin to play a more dominant role. How will you respond to those variables? Certainly not by abandoning that which has brought you so much success, your baby's routine.

You must now become principle-minded, learning how to rightly respond to the emerging variables of your pretoddler's life. This is done by knowing what to expect, when to expect it, and at what ages different patterns of behavior will normally emerge into mature forms. Knowing the progressive nature of growth and development enables a parent to set standards of expected behavior and provide the guidance needed to reach behavioral goals.

What behavior can and should you expect from your pretoddler? Feeding time for your pretoddler is now more than a response controlled by a sucking reflex. For the pretoddler, mealtime is part of a very complex conscious interaction between what the child does and what his parents expect him to do. Right and wrong behaviors will be encouraged, discouraged, and guided when necessary. In fact, right and wrong patterns of behavior will now be part of your baby's entire day. That is why feeding time, waketime, and bedtime provide wonderful opportunities for training.

This series will emphasize the importance of establishing learning patterns——right learning patterns. Those patterns form learning structures that assist the child throughout his early development. As cartilage strengthens and turns into bone, so also learning patterns develop and form the infrastructure of future moral and academic learning. Therefore, the first patterns established best be the right patterns. Researchers and educators agree that growth and development take place in stages, with new experiences building on previous associations. *BABYWISE II* is designed to assist parents in establishing the right patterns of learning, leading to the right infrastructure in an orderly fashion.

This series is not written for the general public but for *BABYWISE* graduates. Your PDF baby has already attained equilibrium in developmental areas, while the demand-fed and attachment-parenting babies usually lag way behind in states of disequilibrium. For that reason we discourage parents from attempting to play catch up with their pretoddler through this series if they have not yet mastered the foundations of the first series. As was the case with *BABYWISE*, we can give you principles but not every possible application. It is vital that you think principle.

The next ten months are critical. The stakes are high. From this point forward you are going after the heart of your child. Many parents place a greater emphasis on the child's psychological health than on his moral health. Parental preoccupation with psychological nurturing is not the medicine for the problem; too often, it is the problem itself, producing emotionally fragile children. Moral health, with an emphasis on heart training, is the medicine preventing emotional deficiencies. This series will advance that cause for you.

In the back of this book we added three appendices: Appendix A: *Child Language Development;* Appendix B: *Teach Your Child to Sign*; Appendix C: *Thoughts on Potty Training*. Read these appendices at your leisure.

Happy pretoddler parenting.

Gary Ezzo, M.A.

Chapter One
Back to Basics

In our first series, *On Becoming BABYWISE,* we stressed the importance of establishing a right mindset for parenting. In *BABYWISE II* we will stress the importance of maintaining that mindset as your baby approaches his first birthday. The most important forces shaping a child's developing personality are those surrounding him in the early years. Parents are a young child's whole world. Therefore, before moving forward, we must first return to some of the foundational principles that brought you to your first level of success. They include (1) *understanding the priority of marriage,* (2) *the dangers of child-centered parenting,* and (3) *knowing how to avoid extremism in the parenting process.* Let's review the basics.

THE PRIORITY OF MARRIAGE
Marriage represents a special bond between two people matched by no other relationship. At least, that was the original idea. Marriage is unique, without parallel, and transcends all other relationships. How amazing it is!

Great marriages make great parents.

A healthy husband-wife relationship is essential to the emotional health of a child. When there is harmony in that relationship, there is an infused stability within the family. A strong marriage provides a haven of security for children as they grow in the nurturing process. Strong marriages create a sense of certainty for children. When a child observes the special friendship and emotional togetherness of his parents, he is more secure simply because he does not have to question the legitimacy of their commitment to one another.

How amazing it is to realize that children have a type of radar device that hones-in on parental conflict. When a child perceives more weakness than strength in his parents' relationship, a low-level anxiety results, ultimately putting a strain on every other learning discipline the child experiences. A child knows intuitively, as his own parents knew when growing up, that if something happens to Mom and Dad, his whole world will collapse. If the parents' relationship is in question in the mind of a child, then that child will live his life on the brink of collapse.

When the marriage relationship is made beautiful, what impressionable child would not want to part of the family? When two are beautifully one, what child would not seek the comforts of your togetherness? The best years of your parenting flow out of the best years of marriage. Protect your marriage!

DANGERS OF CHILD-CENTERED PARENTING
Child-centered parenting threatens successful family life. Listed below are five dangers associated with this style of family government.

1. Child-centered parenting attacks the husband-wife relationship by reducing its practical significance. In marriage, neither men nor women can lose themselves. Marriage forces revelation. We are revealed for what we are. Child-centered parenting wrongly authorizes one or the other to pull away. We are less revealed in parenting, thus less honest about who we are. Attempting to avoid the truth about ourselves, we conveniently find in the name of fatherhood and motherhood a more pleasing image. Whenever we pull away from marriage, no matter how noble the goal, we leave our accountability——our mate. Your children deserve the best from the two of you.

2. Child-centered parenting reverses the natural process of moral development by prematurely creating within a child a false sense of self-reliance. The child becomes, in his thinking, self-sufficient prior to the establishment of needed self-control. That happens because the philosophy grants freedoms beyond the child's ability to manage those freedoms. Self-reliance apart from self-discipline is a destructive influence on young children.

3. Child-centered parenting fosters *family independence,* not *family interdependence.* Children who perceive themselves to be the center of the family universe too often grow into selfish independence. Family independence (rather than family interdependence) becomes a way of life——a lonely one. Independence robs a child of the opportunity to invest in relationships. Where there is no relational invest-

ment, there is no reason for family loyalty. Other people (parents, siblings, and peers) matter only to the extent that advantages are gained by maintaining relationships. What the child can get out of relationships, rather than what he can give, forms the basis of his loyalty. Child-centered parenting fosters that conclusion.

4. Child-centered parenting magnifies the conflict between the *natural way of the child* and his need for moral conformity. Child-centered parenting creates propensities toward negative behavior that will either force the parent and child into an adversarial relationship or force parents to abandon any reasonable standard of moral accountability.

5. Child-centered parenting is reactive, not proactive. Reacting to crises in a child's life is inferior to preventing them.

Now that your baby is here, you can see how easily child-centered parenting can creep into your day. You avoided *demand feeding,* but were you as successful at avoiding *demand attention,* which is the precursor to child-centered parenting? The infant's total dependence on parental care heightens the gratification of the parenting experience. Fortunately, parents can avoid both outcomes. You can meet all your baby's physical and emotional needs and not be child-centered. Here are a few reminders from *BABYWISE* that can help you maintain the balance.

1. Remind yourself that life does not stop once you

have a baby. It may slow up for a few weeks, but it does not stop completely. When you become a mother, you do not stop being a daughter, a sister, a friend, and most importantly, a wife. Those relationships were important to you before the baby. Be sure to maintain them afterwards.

2. If you had a weekly date night with your spouse before the baby was born, continue that practice, letting friends or relatives watch your baby. If you did not have one, start now. Your date does not have to be an expensive or late evening. A child does not suffer from separation anxiety when Mom is with Dad. The marriage relationship is the starting point of security for children.

3. Do not stop doing those special gestures for each other that you once did before children came into your lives. If there was a special activity you both enjoyed previously, plan it into your schedule. If a husband brings home a gift for the baby, he should also bring flowers for his wife. The idea here is basic——continue to do those loving gestures that marked your relationship as special and keep it special.

4. Practice *couch time.* When the workday is over, take 15 minutes and sit on the couch together as a couple. That event should take place when your children are awake, not after bedtime. Explain to your children the importance of having no unnecessary interruptions, because this is a special time for the two of you. Dad will play afterward, but Mom comes first.

Couch time provides a visual sense of your togetherness. In this tangible way children can measure their mom and dad's love relationship and have that inner need satisfied. In addition, couch time provides a predictable forum for a couple to share their relational needs with each other.

5. Invite friends over for a meal or for an evening of companionship. Focusing on hospitality is a healthy distraction from the rigors of childrearing. It obligates you to plan your child's day around serving other people rather than just your child.

6. Parenting is a team sport. It maximizes your collective insights so you can understand your children better and train them properly. As the primary caregiver, Mom must consider it her duty to keep Dad updated on what she is observing. Don't make the mistake of keeping information from your husband, by intent or neglect.

If you desire excellence in parenting, work continually at protecting your marriage. A right perspective about the significance of that relationship is the starting point for healthy parent-child relationships.

PARENTING EXTREMISM AND CONTEXT
As stated in BABYWISE, it is important that you stay centered and avoid the extremes of parenting. That truth must abide throughout your childrearing years. Mothers and fathers that parent in the extremes create prohibitions by elevating their personal approach above what is best given unique circumstances. That is, they elevate the

rule of behavior above the principle that the rule represents. This form of extreme parenting is appropriately titled *legalism.*

We have all heard the phrase, "Let's keep things in context." The most notable aspect of a legalist is that he or she rejects context. Responding to the context of a situation does not mean suspending the principles of *BABYWISE.* Rather, you can focus on the right response in the short term without compromising your long-term objectives.

There will be times when the context of a situation will dictate a temporary suspension of some general guidelines. We desire to stress our position again: As a parent you are endowed with experience, wisdom, and common sense. Trust those attributes first, not an extreme of emotion or the rigidity of the clock. When special situations arise, allow context to guide you. Here are some examples of context, flexibility, and your growing child:

1. You are on an airplane and your six month old begins to fuss loudly. You just fed him two hours ago. What should you do? If neither you nor a toy can satisfy him, consider offering a feeding. The context and ethics involved require that you do not let your baby's routine disturb the flight for everyone else. Failure to act will stress the parent and the rest of the passengers. Although you normally would not feed him so soon after his last feeding, the context of the situation dictates that you suspend your normal routine. When you arrive at your destination, get back to your basic routine. (For more information on traveling with your baby, please see Chapter Seven.)

2. You and your ten month old are staying overnight in the home of a friend. Your son is characterized by sleeping through the night but now begins to wake at 3:00 a.m. What is the morally correct action to take? Pacify the child and help him return to sleep. Yes, at home he may fall back to sleep in five minutes with a little bit of fussing or crying, but you're not at home——you are a guest in someone else's home, and your child is disturbing the sleep of others. When you get home, get back to your basic routine, and your child will follow suit.

Most of your day will be routine and predictable. But there will be times when you may apply more flexibility due to unusual circumstances. Your life will be less tense if you consider the context of each situation and respond appropriately for the benefit of everyone.

SUMMARY

Man is by nature a social creature——both in the broader context of the community in which he lives his public life and in the narrower context of the intimacy of his private world. Man needs someone with whom he can share life, be complete, and have emotional, physical, and spiritual intimacy. All this adds up to marriage and the need to protect it. Child-centered parenting and legalism do not serve marriage or your children. They are plagues; avoid them.

QUESTIONS FOR REVIEW

1. What happens when a child perceives more weakness than strength in his parents' relationship?

   The child feels ~~insecure~~ anxious, when a marriage is weak + unstable, the child's world is also unstable. Strength in a marriage helps the child feel secure + helps foster a good developmental climate

2. How does child-centered parenting reverse the natural process of moral development? Explain.

   ① attack the marriage relationship
   ② creates self-reliance before self-discipline
   3. fosters family independence not interdependence
   4 can cause adversarial relationship c parents.
   5 child centered parenting is reactive not pro-active

3. Why is couch time so important?

   Couch time is important because it enables Hannah to see the togetherness of us. It also allows us a chance to talk.

4. What do parenting extremists create?

Cranky, stressed kids +

Cranky stressed out
parents

5. What does a legalist reject? Explain.

The context. Legalists tend to go by
the clock + let nothing interfere.
They don't take into account the
situation.

Chapter Two
Moral Foundations

Throughout your baby's first year of life, two processes continue to dominate: *growth* and *learning*. These activities are interdependent, but not interchangeable. Growth refers to the biological processes of life; learning refers to the mental processes, which include moral training and development. With both growth and learning, the building blocks are progressive. Each stage of development depends on the successful completion of the previous stage.

FACTORS OF GROWTH
Every specie, whether animal or human, follows a pattern of development peculiar to that species. In postnatal development, infants demonstrate two growth patterns: vertically from head down to feet, and horizontally from the central axis of the body toward the extremities.

Descending vertical development means that amelioration in structure and function come first to the child's head region, then to the child's trunk, and last to his legs and feet. Your baby first started by lifting his head, bobbing it a little, and then letting it fall back to the mattress. Next, he could hold his head upright as a result of his developing neck and chest muscles. At the age of twenty weeks, he had control over the muscles of his eyes, head, and shoulders, but his trunk was still so limp that he had to be propped up or strapped in a chair to be able to maintain a sitting position. He makes good use of his arms and hands in reaching and grasping before he uses his legs. Eventually, he motored himself around by creeping, then crawling, and then walking, running, jumping, and skipping.

Horizontal development proceeds from simple to complex. Growth in the prenatal state starts with the head region and descends to the trunk. Those regions are well developed before the limbs begin to grow. Gradually, the arms lengthened and then developed into the hands and fingers. Functionally, in the postnatal state, a baby will use his chest muscles first, then his arms, and then hands. He will use his hands as a unit before he can control the movements of his fingers. Order is the operative word for biological maturation.

FACTORS OF LEARNING

Whereas biological maturation refers to changes in physical capabilities that result from genetic cues, learning signifies changes resulting from interaction with one's environment, i.e., parental influence and instruction. Like adults, children interpret new experiences in relationship to knowledge formerly acquired. That means learning is progressive, and a child only gains understanding when new information has meaning in relationship to previous experiences. Routine and orderly transition at each stage of the child's development aid the marriage between new information and a child's understanding.

Allowing a child to progress into his new and expanding world in a orderly fashion greatly enhances learning. It is gradual assimilation of many perceptions that gives rise to the formation of ideas. The child that can associate right meanings with new experiences is far more advanced in his understanding than the child that must associate a new meaning to an old situation in need of correction. Since learning comes in progressive stages, training should be equally progressive. Therefore the duty of parents is to channel the child into a learning environment that matches information with understanding.

There are many factors that influence learning both positively and negatively. The child's temperament, the presence or absence of siblings, parental resolve, the purpose for training, the method of instruction, and reinforcement are some of the more obvious factors. Generally speaking, there are three categories of learning: basic skills, academics, and moral development.

Skills

Not all behavior is moral in nature——some actions are morally neutral, such as those related to basic skills. One of the most important and rapid areas of development during the early years of a child's life is motor-skill development. Learning to use a spoon, to walk, swim, tie a shoelace, ride a bike, kick a ball, and climb a rope are nonmoral stage-acquired activities. They are skills associated to a large extent with the child's environment, opportunities to learn, and his motivation to do so. From the helpless state of infancy, skills development continues. Most children learn these feats in progressive stages. When a toddler throws a ball, he does so with his whole body. As his coordination develops, he will throw the ball with just his arm.

Skills, talents, and giftedness are not the same. Skills, for example, are basic to all human beings——such as learning to walk, coloring within the lines, riding a bike, learning to swim, and throwing a ball. Natural talents differ from skills in that they are discriminatory. Everyone has talents, but not necessarily the same talents. Giftedness is a magnified talent. Many musicians are naturally talented, but Mozart was gifted.

Academic Learning

Academic learning is the accumulation of data and the ability to apply logic to given situations. Academic learning, similar to physical development, moves from general to specific and is progressive. We teach our children the alphabet so they can put letters together to form words, then read those words. They first learn to count 1, 2, 3, 4, 5; but it will be a while before they realize that those numbers also represent 12,345. Children first learn about trees in general, then begin to distinguish the pine from the oak, and more specifically, to distinguish the different varieties of pine trees.

Moral Development

While academic training is important, it is by no means mutually exclusive from moral training. At birth, a child has no functioning conscience. By that we mean that he possesses no awareness of standards of right and wrong.

Right from the start, parents should strive to raise a child who regulates his own behavior from within and in accordance to the rules of common ethics. Until the child internalizes healthy moral principles, parents are obligated to make value judgments and moral decisions on behalf of the child. In early parenting, this means that external pressure is necessary to bring about acceptable behavior even though the child has no cognitive understanding of the reason for the behavior. The fact that a child has no moral understanding as to why food should not be intentionally dropped from his high chair does not mean we hold back instructions and restrictions.

With adults, beliefs precede actions; with children, the opposite is true——actions precede beliefs. Parents should insist on moral behavior long before the child is capable of understanding moral concepts. Children first learn how to act morally and then they learn how to think morally. Thus, the two phases of moral training include: (1) *the development of moral behavior,* and (2) *the development of moral concepts.* Actions come first, understanding comes second. This series considers only the importance of moral behavior.

MORAL AND SELF-CONTROL TRAINING

What constitutes moral behavior in pretoddlers? Probably more than you think. The fact that infants do not make moral choices does not mean moral training is not taking place. It is! The first step toward moral comprehension is the development of healthy learning patterns. Structure and your baby's basic routine enhance those patterns. When a child is at peace with his basic environment, his learning potential increases and learning disorders are minimized. In contrast, infants reared by the immediate gratification style of parenting develop unhealthy learning patterns.

Timely gratification training leads to greater self-control in children, which then leads to longer attention spans and thus an advanced aptitude for academic and moral learning. The operative word is *self-control.* Self-control is a base virtue. That is, other virtues are dependent on it. Self-control influences kindness, gentleness, proper speech, controlling negative emotions, concentrating, focusing, sitting skills, and many other behaviors. When you train your child to a right moral response, you simultaneously train him in self-control.

This is a major fork in the road in behavioral studies. Many theorists accept human reason as the basis of morality and focus on intellectual stimulation as a priority above moral development. We invite the reader to consider the opposite. Moral education should not only be a priority of early training, but is absolutely necessary for optimum intellectual achievement.

Why is that true? Because self-control is not an academic discipline, it's a moral one. Sitting, focusing, and concentrating are also moral disciplines borrowed by the intellect to advance academic achievement. At nine months of age, Ashley began to arch her back defiantly while sitting in the high chair. Her actions were moral and her parents' response was moral. Her parents worked to eliminate that behavior, and she learned to sit still by eleven months of age. She was trained so that when she wanted more food or wanted to get down, she would sign with her hands. Because nine-month-old babies are cognitively able to communicate, but not yet verbally capable of doing so, signing became the acceptable form of communication in contrast to arching her back.

What was most significant about her training was not the signing itself, but the level of Ashley's self-control. The self-control she used to not arch her back and the self-control she used to correctly communicate her wishes were one in the same. No training in moral self-control is ever isolated. The self-control needed to sit, think, and choose a better way to communicate is the same self-control that will safeguard the child through life. Such self-control is the product of moral training and not the result of doing flash cards, playing educational games, or learning baby math. There was a moral reason for Ashley to learn self-control, even though she was not cognitive of that reason.

Waiting until a child is five years old is much too late to start working on the skills of sitting, focusing, and concentrating. These are moral developmental skills, not stage-acquired activities. They are skills that are dependent on orderly structure from the earliest days of life. Even now during your baby's first year of life, you are laying the foundations for future development.

Can parents alter their child's intelligence quotient? No. Can they maximize or limit it? Yes. We maintain this perspective because we have consistently found that parents who rejected structure in the early years and who did nothing to correct a lack of structure in the toddler years had actually slowed and, in many cases, corrupted the process of moral and intellectual development. That is why *BABYWISE II* focuses on the heart of the child—— that portion of our humanity from which the issues of life flow. Parents who work on the heart will ultimately train the whole child. Those who work exclusively on the intellect will, at best, raise a smart but morally weak child.

PARENTING INSIDE THE FUNNEL

Please take note of the funnel analogy displayed below. The long stem represents the early stages of parenting, the wider represents growth, maturity, and gradual freedoms. As the child grows up through the stem, freedoms are earned to the extent that responsible behavior is demonstrated.

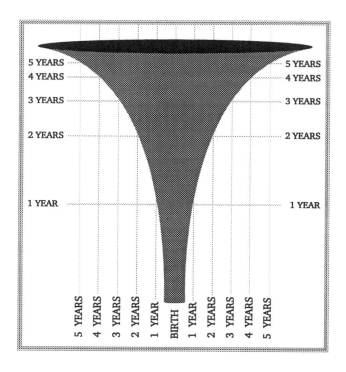

A common mistake is to parent outside of the funnel in the pretoddler months. By "outside the funnel," we mean parents allow behaviors that are neither age-appropriate nor in harmony with the child's moral and intellectual capabilities. To allow a seven month old freedoms belonging to a two year old, or a one year old freedoms belonging to a five year old is to parent outside the funnel. Such freedoms do not facilitate healthy learning patterns. Freedom granted without the guides of self-control ultimately leads a child to enslavement to his passions. The desire for developmental harmony requires that freedoms granted equal age-appropriate self-control. When freedoms granted are greater or less than the child's self-control capacities, a state of developmental disequilibrium is created. Please consider the following basic equations.

1. Freedoms > self-control = developmental confusion
2. Freedoms < self-control = developmental frustration
3. Freedoms = self-control = developmental harmony

With the first, freedoms granted greater than a child's self-control produces developmental confusion. With the second, freedoms withheld a child who possesses age-appropriate self-control will foster developmental frustration. Third, developmental harmony is achieved when freedoms awarded a child are in harmony with his self-control. The following scenario further illustrates these concepts.

Jim and Sally Brown were excited about the mobility of their crawling nine-month-old son Stevie. So as not to stifle his exploration, they put no limitations on him. He had the freedom to touch and explore anything at will. But what happens when the Smith family visits the home of friends or relatives, or visits the store, and Stevie touches all items in sight? How will they restrain him? How will he perceive those restraints? All of a sudden, limitations are placed on a behavior that had no previous limitations. That is more than confusing to the child. It creates an unnecessary adversarial conflict between himself and his parents. No child wants to give up territory once he has gained it.

The problem started when Stevie's parents failed to set age-appropriate boundaries during the early days of his mobility. Because of the lack of restraint, Stevie's mobility put him in an environment larger than he could manage. The excess freedom created too many new variables that he was not ready to handle. Jim and Sally parented outside the funnel. They should have limited his field of exploration by setting appropriate boundaries, training to those boundaries, and then allowing restraint to give way to freedom. Instead they reversed the process, forcing freedom to give way to restraint since Stevie was not able to rightly interact with his environment. Rather than moving him forward gradually to freedom, his parents had to move him backward to restraint. A failure to correct today will lead to moral tyranny tomorrow.

Certainly there will be times when a parent will recall a prematurely granted freedom because the child is not ready to handle the associated responsibilities. Recalling privileges should not be the norm but the exception in your parenting. You can help yourself avoid reparenting by evaluating what you allow your child to play with or to do. For example, do you let your eight month old play with the television remote control? If yes, why? Does he understand what it's used for, how it works, or why it's not a toy? When he begins to bang it on the coffee table, will you take it away? When he begins to bang it on the neighbor's coffee table, how will you restrain him? What are you going to do when he resists you taking possession of it? All of a sudden you are surrounded by variables that should never have been part of your baby's life. Letting your child play with the television remote control is parenting outside the funnel. At this age, it has no meaning or purpose. Why add a variable to his life that will only need correction later? Allowing a child unlimited freedom of exploration is developmentally unwise and unhealthy. Freedom is not the problem: it's the child's inability to handle the power of freedom.

Here is another example. Rebecca's parents found it amusing to watch her tear up old newspapers. She enjoyed this seemingly benign form of entertainment. But why allow that behavior at all? Besides being dangerous, the fun of tearing paper leads to the fun of tearing pages out of books——Mom's, Dad's, and the baby's. Then what will you do? Not only must you correct the behavior, but now the child has limited access to educational opportunities gained from her books. These examples are representative of parenting outside the funnel. In both cases, reparenting must take place.

To avoid reparenting, which is usually less than satisfactory, you should continually evaluate what you allow your child to do given his age, understanding, and abilities. Are you giving him inappropriate freedoms? Parent the constant factors and control the variables until the child has the moral capacity to handle the freedom those variables bring. The twelve month old who at nine months of age learned his boundaries and how to respond to his parents' voice limitations will have many more freedoms at home and away than the child who had the freedoms early but lost them because of unmanageable behavior. Life for you and your baby will be much more manageable and pleasurable when you parent within the funnel, allowing restraint to give way to freedoms.

SUMMARY

As a parent you are obligated to produce a responsible human being, and that challenge should not be left up to chance. Accept the challenge of parenting, realizing the process of training starts with you. Belonging to your family is not an option for your child, but a mandate. That means moral conformity is required. There are certain virtues worth acquiring, such as kindness, goodness, gentleness, charity, honesty, honor, and respect. Since these qualities are not naturally found in a child's life, they must be instilled and nurtured into his heart.

You are the governors of your child's life. Be proud of that fact. Do not shy away from it. You are to govern it until he develops within his heart the self-control and the moral precepts that will allow him to govern himself. Self-legislative freedoms come gradually——from the playpen, to the backyard, to the neighborhood. As your child demonstrates age-responsible behavior and sound judgment, he earns another level of freedom. This type of training results in a developmentally healthy child who is a joy to everyone.

QUESTIONS FOR REVIEW

1. Briefly describe the three categories of learning.

   a. Skills - Motor skills, creeping, crawling, walking. spoon fork,

   b. academics - building blocks of knowledge

   c. Moral

2. What are two phases of moral training?

Moral behavior - actions learning self-control, focusing, being able to sit still.

Moral Beliefs - the reasons behind moral behavior.

3. Why is self-control so important?

Self-control is important because it enables the child to focus, sit still, learn. Self control applies to all aspects of life. As children learn self-control, they use this skill to rise to higher levels of development in academic areas.

4. Explain why moral education should not only be a priority of early training, but is absolutely necessary for optimum intellectual achievement.

Moral education is necessary because it aids in further intellectual achievement. Moral education must be consistent from the earliest ages.

5. Explain how the funnel analogy is rightly and wrongly used.

    The funnel analogy is rightly used when parents structure + routine enables the child to grow in an age appropriate environment. freedom = self control = harmony

6. What is implied by the phrase "parenting outside the funnel"?

    Given children freedoms that are age inappropriate

Chapter Three
Mealtime Activities

In *BABYWISE*, we introduced the three activities of your baby's day——feeding time, waketime, and naptime. With age-appropriate modifications, those activities continue right into the toddler years. Your baby's first year is divided into four basic phases: phase one: *Stabilization;* phase two: *Extended Night*; phase three: *Extended Day*; and phase four: *Extended Routine.* The focus of this chapter is on feeding times and related mealtime activities associated with the fourth phase, extended routine (six months and beyond).

By six months of age, PDF babies make the transition from a four-hour routine to three meals a day (breakfast, lunch, and dinner) with one additional liquid feeding offered at bedtime. (If nursing, the last feeding is necessary to maintain your milk supply.) You will supplement the three main meals with baby food. Eventually, you may add an afternoon snack when five or six hours separate lunch from dinner.

PRAYER

We believe that life is more than a cosmic accident without rhyme or reason. The existence of a personal, benevolent, orderly God is part of our world view. If it is part of yours, then consider offering a prayer of thanks at each mealtime. Parents act as proxies for their children in several different ways. We are to serve as their moral consciences until theirs are fully developed. We make wise decisions on their behalf until they grow in wisdom. And we offer thanks on their behalf for the food they are about to receive. The first eternal truth your child will participate in is touching the throne of God with prayer. Pray with your children, especially at mealtime. The early establishment of healthy prayer patterns is important. Verbally giving thanks sets an example that honors God. When you pray with him, hold his little hand and say, "Let's bow our heads and thank God." What a blessing it will be to have a child who at fifteen months of age voluntarily waits before he eats until a prayer of thanks is offered.

INTRODUCING SOLID FOODS

Parent-directed feeding continues in the pretoddler months with the addition of solid foods. Parents usually introduce solids to their babies when they are between the ages of four to six months. Your pediatrician will advise you when to start your child on solids. Factors influencing when to start food supplements include the age of the baby, his weight gain, and his sleep patterns. The introduction of solids does not mean the suspension of liquid feedings. The calories gained from breast milk or formula are still of primary importance. Neither solid nor liquid feedings are nutritionally sufficient alone.

Getting Started

Mothers are naturally concerned about the nutritional health of their babies and often ask questions like: "What do I feed my baby?" "What if he doesn't like it?" "How does feeding solids fit with his daily routine?" and, "Where do I begin?" One guide to remember is this: Many of the common-sense nutritional principles that apply to you as an adult apply to your baby.

Initially, you should offer your baby his solids at the normal feeding times. For example, if you have been feeding him at 7:00 a.m. (breakfast), 11:00 a.m. (lunch), 3:00 p.m. (dinner), and 7:00 p.m., then solids should accompany the three major meals. Continue to offer the breast or bottle before serving solids. Your goal by the end of your child's sixth month is to align his mealtimes with those of the rest of the family.

Breast-feeding mothers should maintain four nursing periods a day for adequate milk supply. Begin feeding your baby with one breast. Offer the solids next, followed by the other breast. If you find that your baby is not taking the solids well, experiment by offering some solids first, then offer the breast, offer solids again, and then finish on the breast. With bottle feeding, offer half a bottle, then the solids, then the remaining bottle.

NOTE: Do not offer solids, then two hours later nurse, followed two hours later with more solids. That's snacking, not eating, and will disrupt your child's hunger and sleep/wake stabilization.

Even at mealtime, stay mindful of training so as to avoid retraining. Do not allow poor eating habits such as fingers in the mouth, playing with food, and spitting food out to become a normal pattern of your child's behavior. It only means correcting him at a later date. To help him become better coordinated with a spoon or fork, allow him to play with a spoon during bath time, not meal time. As he moves to more textured foods (Cheerios, peas, bananas, and finger foods), offer him the appropriate utensil. The child will naturally use whatever is easiest. Initially, this means his fingers, but in time (usually by eighteen to twenty-four months), he will master both spoon and fork. Be patient! Learning to hold these utensils properly is a motor skill and is part of his normal growth process.

Introducing Cereal

When introducing cereal to your baby's diet, start with *your* most convenient feeding of the day. Be patient with the process. Placing a spoon in the mouth of a four or five month old is not only a new experience but is equally a foreign one for your baby. Your baby will initially tongue thrust the food right back out——not because he doesn't like it, but he doesn't know what to do with it. Taking food from a spoon is usually mastered in three or four days.

By the second week, you can offer rice cereal at breakfast, lunch, and dinner. (Other cereal mixes such as oatmeal, barley, or wheat can be introduced to your baby's diet after vegetables and fruits are successfully introduced. Check with your pediatrician for the recommended timetable for adding other cereals.) Start by mixing one tablespoon of rice cereal with four to five tablespoons of breast milk or formula. Initially, the consistency will be thin, but not so thin as to run off the spoon. Gradually increase the amount of cereal from five to eight tablespoons, thickening the consistency. You can start introducing vegetables two weeks later. Because cereal is such an excellent source of iron, we suggest you continue at least one serving a day up to a year.

Introducing Vegetables

Your baby should receive three cereal portions a day for two weeks before starting him on vegetables. Each meal must be supplemented with a liquid feeding. The following suggestions (not rules) may be helpful when it is time to introduce vegetables to your baby's diet. Start with the noon meal, introducing yellow vegetables (squash and carrots) first. A couple of days later offer a different squash. Approximately two weeks later introduce green vegetables (peas and beans), followed two weeks later by fruits.

Each time you introduce another food group (vegetable or fruits), start with a couple of tablespoons, watching for excessive fussiness, diarrhea, rashes, or runny nose, all of which are possible signs of food allergies. Meats should be the last foods offered, and you may hold off until your baby is up to one year of age. Eventually your baby's menu will look similar to this:

Breakfast: Cereal and fruits
Lunch: Vegetables and fruits
Dinner: Cereal, vegetables, and fruits

How much should each serving be? Within reason, allow your baby to set the amounts per serving. Age-appropriate amounts are usually listed on baby-food items. If in doubt, check with your pediatrician's office for suggested guidelines.

Introducing Fruits

Your baby needs the nutrition that comes from vegetables. Fruits are not a substitute for them. For your convenience, mix your baby's fruit portions with his cereal. Be careful about the order of servings. Because fruits are naturally sweet, children prefer them to cereal or vegetables. Therefore, we suggest you offer your vegetables first, then your fruit-flavored cereal.

Making Your Own Baby Food

Preparing your own baby food is an easy, money-saving alternative to store bought brands. For example, one bag of carrots (59 cents) will yield four to six jars of prepared baby food. The average cost of store brands is 45 cents per jar.

It is easy to prepare vegetables such as carrots, peas, green beans, yams, sweet potatoes, and butternut squash, and they freeze well. To prepare carrots, peas, and green beans, boil them in water until tender. Puree in a blender, adding small amounts of purified water as needed. To prepare yams, sweet potatoes, and squash, oven cook them until very soft. Remove the skin and seeds, then puree the remainder in a blender with purified water. When preparing large quantities for freezing, always sterilize your containers. When needed, thaw the food in your refrigerator. Your cookbook is a good resource for baby food preparation.

Finger Foods

High chair finger foods are just that——finger foods and not a cereal paste. Acts of self-feeding are dependent on the maturation of the *grasping reflex*. When your baby's thumb and forefinger grasp develops to the point that he can pick up a Cheerio (usually around eight months), then he is ready for finger foods. It is interesting to watch a baby get started with self-feeding. His little fingers find a piece of food, grasp it, take it to his mouth, and then he uses his whole hand to shovel it in. In time, he will master the skill of placing food in his mouth with just his fingers. Parents may encourage finger-food eating but should realize also that it is a transitional skill. It assists the child in the transition from feeding dependence to feeding independence with the aid of a utensil.

Juices

Fruit juice is a friendly liquid alternative to your baby's diet but not a substitute meal. By that we mean that it is not a replacement for breast milk or formula, nor does a child need juice every day.

The introduction of juices to your baby's diet should begin around six months of age. We recommend offering the clear juices (apple, grape, cranberry, etc.) first. After your baby's first year, you can introduce the pulp juices (orange, grapefruit, etc). Because of their sweetness, you should dilute the clear juices with water by 50%. The diluting practice can continue until his second birthday. At six months start with three diluted ounces per day, and over the next six months work up to six ounces per day.

Initially parents should limit juices to mealtimes, offering them in a sippy cup but not in a bottle. In fact, we suggest you avoid offering juices from the bottle altogether. That obviously includes putting a child down for a nap with a bottle of juice. In a reclining position, the juice sugars can collect easily and decay baby teeth. After your child's first birthday, a juice drink makes a good snack. You can offer it to your baby after he wakes up from his afternoon nap, or when he's out shopping with Mom.

Snacks

Some pediatricians recommend introducing juice and finger-food snacks by the age of six months. Snacks are a fun treat but like anything else, balance is needed. A snack is not a second meal. How will you know if you're offering too many snacks? Your child will eat poorly at the next meal or become a picky eater. If you see that happening, cut back on the amount of snacks offered or cut them out all together. Here are a few helpful hints about snacking.

1. You may not have to offer a snack every day.

2. Use moderation. Do not let snacks detract from a hearty appetite.

3. Do not use food to avoid conflict.

4. As your child stays awake longer, avoid using food as a pacifier.

5. The place for snacking should be consistent, such as an infant seat or high chair. Avoid allowing your child to crawl or walk around the house or store with a juice drink or snack in his hand.

6. As a general suggestion, offer snacks in the afternoon, such as after your child wakes up from his nap.

The Finicky Eater

Like all people, your baby will show preferences in taste, so do not be too quick to say, "Oh, he doesn't like it." While you will occasionally give him what he likes, you must also consider what meets the needs and desires of the entire family. When age-appropriate, offer him foods that your family normally eats.

Many finicky eaters are created not born. As a parent, evaluate your relationship to food. Are you overly concerned with nutritional intake, a picky eater yourself, or a junk-food connoisseur? As hard as it may be, try not to pass on any extreme preoccupations with food. Family mealtime and the kitchen table should not become a war zone. Try to make meals a pleasant experience for all. Here are some age-appropriate suggestions.

For children under six months: When possible, place your baby in his infant seat near the dinner table. Sight and family sounds are important to the establishment of early family identity. There will be some occasions when mealtime for the rest of the family will be playpen time for the baby.

Six to twelve months (or until the child can feed himself):

[49]

At this age, your baby may actually eat his main meal before the rest of the family sits down. Then, while the rest of the family enjoys their meal together, the baby can sit in his high chair with some finger foods. Now everyone is participating, and Mom gets to enjoy her meal as well.

Twelve months and older: Family mealtime should be characterized by everyone eating together. To keep the evening meal pleasant, put more concentrated effort into highchair problems at breakfast and lunch. That does not mean you will not correct during dinner, but the concentrated effort at the other meals can speed up the process of dining harmony.

WEANING YOUR BABY
Weaning, by today's definition, is the process by which parents offer food supplements in place of, or in addition to, mother's milk. That process begins the moment the parents give their baby formula, or when he first tastes cereal. From that moment on, weaning is a gradual process.

From the Breast

The duration of breast feeding has varied in extreme from birth to fifteen years. No one can say for sure what age is ideal. For some it may be six months, for others a year. Breast-feeding for more than a year is a matter of preference since adequate supplementary food is usually available. During biblical times, weaning took place between eighteen and twenty-four months; three years was more the exception than the rule.

At birth, infants depend totally on their caregiver to meet their physical needs. But they must gradually become more independent, taking small steps at a time. One such step for your baby is the ability to feed himself. You can start by eliminating one nursing period at a time, going three to four days before dropping the next one. That time frame allows a mom's body to make the proper reductions in milk.

Usually the late-afternoon feeding is the easiest to drop, since it is a busy time of day. Replace each feeding with six to eight ounces of formula or milk (depending on the child's age). Pediatricians generally recommend that parents not give their babies cow's milk until they are at least one year of age. If your baby is nine months old or older, consider going straight to a cup rather than to a bottle. The transition will be easiest if you have introduced the cup prior to weaning.

From the Bottle

When your baby is one year of age, you can begin to wean him from the bottle. Although an infant can become very attached to his bottle, you can minimize that problem by not letting him hold it for extended periods of time. There is a difference between playing with the bottle and drinking from it. You can start to introduce the sippy cup as early as six months. Becoming familiar with it early aids the transition process. The weaning process takes time, so be patient. Begin by eliminating the bottle at one meal, then at another, and so on.

SUMMARY
We might expect that establishing good feeding habits

would be the easiest feature of a child's training. The more established a child's diet and eating routines, based on parental direction and not the free will of the child, the smoother the process goes. Introducing solids to your baby's diet is part of the natural process of growth. Even with the introduction of solids, stay mindful to train the child so as to avoid retraining later.

QUESTIONS FOR REVIEW

1. During the *extended routine* phase of your baby's day, how many times should you feed him?

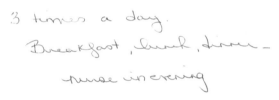

3 times a day.
Breakfast, lunch, dinner -
nurse in evening

2. When should parents normally introduce solids into their baby's diet?

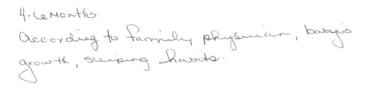

4-6 Months.
According to family physician, baby's
growth, sleeping habits.

3. What wrong feeding habits disrupt your child's hunger patterns and sleep/wake stabilization? Explain.

Nursing, feeding two hrs later, then nursing 2° after that. It teaches the kid to snack.

4. When and how should parents introduce vegetables into their baby's diet?

Start @ the noon meal with yellow vegetables. Try a new yellow vegetable q 3 days. 2 weeks later start ē green vegetables. Then 2 weeks later fruit.

5. What should parents offer a baby first, fruits or vegetables? Explain.

Parents should offer vegetables first. Because fruits are sweet + kids will naturally prefer them.

6. Acts of self-feeding depend on what two factors?

maturation of the grasping reflex.

Chapter Four
Highchair Manners

When you add them all up, your baby spends many hours a week in his high chair. Take advantage of that time by making it an opportunity for learning. As with many aspects of child development, there are both constant and variable influences with which to contend. Parents are the constant influence on moral training. Whether at mealtime, playtime, or roomtime, they should be reinforcing a constant and consistent level of behavioral expectation. For example, the instructions "Do not drop your food" and "Do not touch the stereo" differ only in the nature of the activity, not in the level of expectation. The variable is the place or item of offense, but the constant is the level of expectation. The "no" of the high chair is to be the same "no" of the living room.

Parents of pretoddlers too often isolate individual acts of behavior rather than seeing the need for conformity as part of the same process. Although the settings and activities vary, parents act as the constant influence to bring to each situation the consistency necessary for orderly development and growth.

When a problem occurs at mealtime, consider what other conflicts are present throughout the day. Are they related? Is the problem tied only to food, or does he act similarly in other settings? For example, if he's having problems keeping his hands where they belong while in the high chair, is he also having struggles with touching off-limit items in the living room? The root problem then, is a general lack of self-control and not exclusively a mealtime weakness.

If you demand a standard at mealtime, then the same level of expectation must be in place with other activities. If you demand compliance while in other settings, but not at mealtime, confusion and frustration will result.

SELF-CONTROL TRAINING WITH HANDS

Parents are active participants in their child's advancing cognitive development (putting thoughts in action) and they should not delay training hoping the process will get easier later. Dealing with the problem later usually means backtracking. Train, do not retrain!

Baby and Mom will spend much time together at meals; therefore, consider that time an opportunity to teach basic skills. A baby learns by way of instruction and restriction. For example, instruct your baby in the appropriate use of his hands and his voice, and begin to teach him early table manners. On the restrictive side, do not let him help you put pureed food in his mouth with his hands. The food usually ends up all over his face and in his hair. Also, he does not need to hold the utensil that you're using to feed him. These examples are simple behaviors that need restriction. Bad habits started early will require corrective training later.

If you have to, hold his hands away from the food. Even better, teach him where to place his hands while being fed. You have saved yourself much trouble when your baby masters hand control. Too often, early parental training is reactive and restrictive, not proactive and directive. For example, the child that first puts his hands in his food, then in his hair, and then on his shirt receives correction from his frustrated mother. She then has to restrict the child's actions.

Restricting behavior that was once allowed makes compliance difficult. Train the child and then release him to freedom. Do not allow freedoms that will eventually need restraint. In the previous example, the parent is not managing right behavior but chasing after wrong behavior.

Importance of Verbal Instruction

How much of your instructions does your baby understand? More than you think. Vocabulary comprehension and mastery come in three phases.

The first phase is *understanding vocabulary*. That is, the child understands the meaning of words long before he can verbalize them. Your six month old will wave "bye-bye" or play pattycake upon your encouragement. By eight months of age, he has an enormous understanding of vocabulary and demonstrates it by his responses to instructions such as "come to mama," "sit down," "blow kisses," "hug your baby doll," "see the plane," "touch the kitty," "wave bye-bye," and so on. Your child responds because of his understanding, but he has not yet learned to speak the words he understands.

Speaking vocabulary is the second level of achievement

and usually develops from twelve months of age. Your baby will babble to a toy or sibling. That babbling means something to the child. Those are word-thoughts coming out in scrambled speech.

Reading is the third level of vocabulary achievement. It begins around the age of two and one-half years, when a child begins to recognize and form letters. For an expanded explanation on child language development, see Appendix A.

Your *BABYWISE* baby is ready to learn. While giving verbal instructions, show him concretely what you expect. For example, when you want to teach him where to put his hands during mealtime, take his hands and place them either on the side of the high chair tray or underneath the tray on his lap. You might say, "Put your hands on the side of the tray please," while actually taking his hands and placing them there.

The benefits associated with proper placement of hands become obvious in light of the wrong behaviors that can result without it. Training correctly from the start eliminates the need for correcting wrong behavior later. The more you appropriately train, the less you have to correct. Be patient with your child, but above all, be proactive in the training process.

METHODS OF DISCIPLINE

Parents are responsible for training. The word *train* means to initiate, get started, set the patterns, cause one to learn. The goal of pretoddler training is not to prevent your child from exploring life, but to help him develop healthy behavior patterns so he can learn about life. Those patterns include paying attention, focusing, and concentrating on what he is doing——all basic skills of life. You began the process with your basic routine and will continue the process by encouraging your child in right behavior, correcting wrong patterns of behavior.

In the pretoddler phase of development, behaviors needing correction are initially wrong functionally but not morally. Therefore, we correct wrong patterns and encourage right patterns. Children do not naturally grow into right behavior——they are trained into it.

There will be plenty of opportunities to train while your child sits in the high chair. The right method of correction and the right amount of limitation needed to achieve your goals depends on the age of the child. Common highchair problems are controlled and amended by a combination of the following methods:

1. Verbal reprimand. This requires the exercise of verbal authority.

2. Isolate to the crib. This is removing the child from an act or place of conflict and putting him in his crib. Pretoddlers can learn very quickly cause-and-effect relationships. They can also learn that behavioral expectations are not negotiable.

3. Loss of privilege or toy. This is a logical consequence that also works effectively. The purpose of logical consequences in pretoddler training is to reinforce your verbal instructions.

4. Light to moderate swat on the hand. This measure is for the older, more mobile pretoddler whose hands are touching items he shouldn't. A slight to moderate swat on the hand accompanied by verbal correction is

not a punishment but a deterrent and attention draw-ing technique demonstrating parental resolve on an issue. Swatting a little hand for the express purpose of calling attention to a limitation will not leave your child psychologically scarred, affect his self-esteem, train him to hit other children, teach him violence, or cause him in adulthood to abuse his own children. But it will encourage him to make right decisions.

Spanking, as traditionally practiced in our society, is not an acceptable form of correction during the pretodd-ler phase of development. If it is to be introduced into the life of your child, it will be much later. For now, it is enough to say that the use of verbal reprimands, isola-tion, loss of privilege, and swatting the hand are appro-priate disciplines for the pretoddler phase. As we move through the balance of this chapter, considering the appropriate methods of pretoddler correction, keep in mind your overall objective——helping your child gain age-appropriate self-control.

Your baby's routine in the early months created a cri-tical foundation for the pretoddler phase. In the next six to eight months, parents should fortify that foundation and expand on it to help the child receive the rapid amount of data that bombards him during his socializa-tion stage, fourteen to forty months. Much of your suc-cess during the toddler years will be a result of pre-toddler training. Don't miss the critical opportunities for learning that come during the pretoddler months.

Consider the following high chair problems as oppor-tunities for advanced training. In these early months, conflict resolution is superior to conflict avoidance. The long-term results of right training are wonderful.

Common Highchair Problems

There are a number of different but related highchair behavior problems. Although the type of offense varies, the methods of correction are often the same. Included in the group of highchair violations are:

1. flipping the plate
2. dropping and throwing food
3. playing with food
4. messy hands in the hair
5. banging on the tray
6. standing in the high chair
7. arching the back
8. spitting raspberries
9. screaming

Because these behaviors have common denominators (the high chair and mealtime), they also share a common correction. To demonstrate that, we will take up the first two problems, flipping the plate and the intentional dropping of food from the high chair. When working to correct a new but wrong behavior, a bad habit, or to prevent one from starting, remember that wholesome correction is always consistent. Consistency aids the learning process, especially during the pretoddler stage.

Flipping Plate and Dropping Food from the High Chair

Parents should place finger foods directly on the highchair tray or on a plate. When finger foods are on a plate, one common and curious temptation of a child is to pick up the plate and flip it, spilling all the contents. Do not allow that habit to begin. Mealtime is not playtime. Here a firm "No, do not touch your plate, only your food" is the starting point of training and correcting. If you let the child play with his plate even though he doesn't spill the food, you have granted him an unnecessary freedom that will only nudge him closer to wrong behavior and away from right behavior. There is no developmental advantage gained by your child playing with a plate of food.

Sometimes food is accidentally dropped——for that, guidance, not correction, is necessary. But what about the intentional dropping or throwing of food from the high chair? Those actions need correcting. Some parents go to extremes to avoid conflict rather than train their children in self-control. Believing that simple self-restraining behavior is too much to expect from their child, they allow behavioral freedoms that will need correcting at a later date. We refer to that as "credit-card parenting." You will pay the training price in the future but with compounded interest. Instead of training their children not to drop food, some mothers allow the behavior and minimize damage by manipulating their children's environment.

Inflating a child's rubber swimming pool and placing it under the high chair is one such example. With this trick the child can have fun with his food and the kitchen floor stays clean (until the child learns to throw his food outside the parameters of the pool). Although the parent has successfully avoided conflict (temporarily) by not insisting on a standard, she has also missed a wonderful opportunity to train in self-control. With that style of environmental manipulation, no urgency exists to train a child in appropriate mealtime behavior. Such an approach usually backfires on the parent. The self-control normally learned by properly handling food is the same self-control needed to guide the child in later freedoms. Missed training opportunities result in slower intellectual growth.

It is possible to train your child not to drop his food by giving immediate attention to the offense. First, correct the child verbally, and then if need be, provide an attention getting swat his hand. Finally, isolate him to the crib. The child will fuss over that consequence, but when he is done, bring him back to the high chair and try it again. If the child persists (and some will), mealtime may be over and naptime might begin. One thing is for certain: immediate and consistent consequences speed up the learning process. In the past, educators were concerned with parents who pushed their children too fast. Today, we are concerned with parents who do not push their children enough.

The principles of correction for flipping and dropping food are the same for the rest of the offenses previously listed. For example, the child that plays with his food (mashing it needlessly), stands in his high chair, or bangs his spoon on his tray receives first a verbal reprimand, and if need be, either a swat to the hand (or thigh if standing in the high chair), isolation, or both. Your choices are limited at this age when it comes to corrective methods.

If he is blowing bubbles with his food (commonly referred to as blowing raspberries), then lightly place your finger over his mouth and give a stern "No! Keep your food in your mouth." If further correction is needed, isolation is usually the next step. Stay cognitive of the fact that a pretoddler, especially one who started with *BABYWISE*, responds to these methods of correction with positive results.

Whining

Whining is an unacceptable form of communication that becomes annoying to the listener if left unchecked. Whining is a learned trait, not a warning of deep-seated emotional problems. At what age might whining begin? As soon as your child begins to communicate ideas. Though half-hearted at the outset and not done with rebellious motives, whining will become either a bad habit or a manipulative tool if not attended to early. The most common way parents reinforce this habit is by giving in to it.

Whining prior to fifteen months of age usually reflects a limited vocabulary. For example, if your baby wants more food, he may use a half-cry communication to ask for it. Although this is an expression of whining, it is not a protest or a challenge to authority at this stage. The good news is this: when you rightly deal with highchair whining, you are simultaneously hedging against behavioral whining that comes in the toddler and posttoddler years.

Providing an Alternative

The root of the problem at this age is not the whining, but the lack of communicative alternatives. Children between eight and twelve months of age are cognitively able to communicate, but are not yet verbally capable of doing so.

To prevent whining and to facilitate your child's verbal skills, start around eight months of age to teach your infant how to communicate through sign language. It is never too early to emphasize "please" and "thank you."

Remember, your child's verbal comprehension precedes his verbal vocabulary. You can effectively teach the following phrases: "please," "thank you," "stop," "more food," and "all done." For an expanded explanation on signing, see Appendix B.

Work on one expression at a time, taking the child's hand through the motions while saying the word. Begin with "please," adding the name of the requested item to the end. For example, "Please, more cheese," "Please, more meat," or "Please, more drink." When you sense that your child understands but refuses to say it back, use natural consequences to reinforce the correct response. If he desires more food, do not give him any until he signs "please". If he desires to get down, keep him in his chair. If you find yourself getting into a power struggle, isolate the child rather than giving him the opportunity to challenge you directly. Here are four reasons to teach your baby to sign:

1. You are teaching and reinforcing habits of self-control.

2. It eliminates wrong communicative methods by providing right modes of expression.

3. Signing aids discretionary correction in the future. There will be times when you cannot correct your child publicly or verbally. The silence of signing and Mom's facial expression communicate the same intent as verbal correction.

4. You are actually teaching your child a second language during a time in his life when he is most recep-

tive to language formation.

Take your time, be consistent, and above all, be patient.

SUMMARY
Some parents see as their duty the need to make their children happy, never recognizing that this treatment may deprive their little ones of the strength that comes from wise restrictions and loving corrections. Mealtime behavior provides opportunities for learning and growth in self-control. Do not shy away from the opportunity to train. And remember, early training establishes right patterns of behavior that help advance the child in all future activities.

QUESTIONS FOR REVIEW

1. What is the goal of pretoddler training? What is not the goal?

   The goal of pretoddler training is to help establish learning patterns + self-control.

2. List and describe the three phases of vocabulary comprehension.

   a. *Understanding - the child understands words - Bye, Hello*

   b. *Speaking -*

c. *Reading* -

3. What are the four methods of corrective discipline for pre-toddlers?

   a. Verbal reprimand

   b. isolate to crib

   c. loss of privilege or toy

   d. light to moderate swat on hand.

4. In corrective parenting, what speeds up the learning process?

   Being consistent

5. What is credit-card parenting?

If we don't train our kids now, you have to pay the piper in the future

Chapter Five
Waketime Activities

In the building process, whether it be for a physical structure or the moral fabric of a human heart, it is vital to lay the proper foundation. Unfavorable or inadequate training during the pretoddler phase of development can seriously sabotage physical and mental propensities. That is why the establishment of right patterns of behavior is basic to all human potential. Parents must not only give attention to what is imparted, but also to how it is imparted.

Allowing a child to grow up doing whatever he wishes without placing any conformity demands or limitations on him is obviously not fair to the child. Children need guidance most in the early stages of learning, when the foundations are being laid. If parents set the right course for a child and encourage him to stay on course by their parental administration, he will be less likely to stray and more likely to progress quickly through the process of learning.

The establishment of right patterns of learning from the start plays an increasingly dominant role in the pretoddler's maturation process. Right patterns ultimately affect the way a child manages instruction, direction, correction, limitation, freedom, and new and growing relationships. As he grows, his world develops and becomes increasingly more complicated. Therefore, how a child assimilates knowledge and how he learns to respond to parental cues are foundational to all future growth.

DEVELOPMENTAL DEPRIVATION

The term developmental deprivation does not mean that a child is deprived of opportunities to learn, but of the best opportunities to learn. To a large extent, a child's environment determines his learning patterns. We believe that learning deprivation occurs when parents consider a pretoddler's and toddler's impetuous and momentary desires to be their prime source of learning. For example, allowing a child to crawl or walk around the house unhindered, without any guidelines, directions, or restrictions represents a dubious channel of learning. Learning is too often accidental and outside the context of the pretoddler's developing world.

Suggested by the nonrestrictive theory of allowing a child to explore unhindered is the idea that learning through trial-and-error in a nonstructured environment, with parents acting as *facilitator* of learning rather than *teachers* of knowledge, is a superior training method. Not so! Facilitating a child's learning and teaching a child are two distinctly different approaches. Trial-and-error self-exploration is inferior to structured guidance with proactive teaching. Allowing trial-and-error learning to become the primary source of education even for a pretoddler is time-consuming, and too often the end results are far from satisfactory. Trial-and-error parenting often creates learning environments that are greater than the intellectual capacities of the child, as well as patterns that will need retraining.

Pretoddlers and toddlers need direction and guidance from their parents. They must learn correct, specific responses in specific situations and be able to transfer the concept to other situations. "Do not drop your food" and "Do not touch the stereo" are examples of what we mean. Those actions are different, but the desired response in both cases is the same——in this case, submission to parental instruction. If parents reinforce their instruction in the living room, but not in the kitchen, then the child's ability to discriminate between what his parents expect and what they allow becomes clouded.

PLANNED LEARNING OPPORTUNITIES

Learning opportunities should be predominantly the result of planning——not chance. The establishment of healthy learning patterns is the result of providing the right learning environment, one in which controlled stimuli (those factors that normally call for curiosity and investigation) are part of your baby's day. To achieve this end, plan some structured time into your baby's waketime. Those opportunities will include, (1) *structured playtime alone*; (2) *time with family members*; and (3) *free playtime*.

Structured Playtime Alone

We maintain that play activities serve the learning process. But the spontaneous interest of pretoddlers and toddlers is not the only influence on their play, since parents control to a large extent the environment in which they learn. Therefore, both structured and non-structured learning environments are needed. Structured playtime is a specific time during the day when a child has time to play by himself. It starts in the early months with the playpen and advances to roomtime.

Playpen Time

Many parents regard the use of the playpen as a means of controlling the child's environment for the moment. While that is one usage, it should by no means be the primary function. The long-term benefits resulting from early use of the playpen will show up for years to come. By six months of age, your baby should be taking some naps in his playpen or have slept in it while away from home. The playpen is an essential tool for your child's safety and an effective aid to your child's learning. The playpen fosters the most basic learning skills of life: sitting, focusing, and concentrating.

Why Use a Playpen?

There are several practical benefits from the use of a playpen.

1. It provides a safe environment. Playpens are a safe environment for your baby when your attention must be elsewhere, and it's not his naptime. You can take a shower, unload groceries from the car, care for other children, and do a host of other activities knowing your child is safe.

2. It doubles as a portable bed. The playpen can be a portable bed, which is especially useful when visiting another home. The playpen gives the baby a clean and familiar place to sleep.

3. It offers a structured learning center. Most importantly, your baby's first structured learning takes place in the playpen. The partnership a child has with the playpen establishes foundational intellectual skills. Planned daily playpen times allow little ones the opportunity to develop in many ways.

   a. Mental focusing skills. Playpen time helps a child develop the ability to concentrate on an object or activity at hand and not be distracted constantly.

   b. Sustained attention span. You will observe how your child picks up a toy, manipulates it with his hand, examines it with his eyes, shakes it, and then revisits the process again.

   c. Creativity. Creativity is the product of boundaries, not freedom. With absolute freedom, there is no need for creative thinking or problem solving.

   d. Self-play adeptness. This is one of the positive signs that your baby is moving from dependence to independence.

   e. Orderliness. The first step to developing orderliness is to help your child with clean-up times. Start by placing a few books in one corner, a bucket of small toys in another, or stacking other items in a neat pile. Simple statements such as "Let's put the toys in the basket" or "Help Mommy clean up" aid the process. The object is to leave the area neat, with the child participating in that goal.

If the child misses structured playtime, the repertoire of skills he might otherwise attain by these activities could be seriously delayed.

When to Use the Playpen

Schedule your playpen time at approximately the same hour each day, selecting times when your baby is fresh and alert (not before naptime). Put several interesting toys within his reach or put the toys in a small basket and place the basket in the playpen. Keep the toys age appropriate and occasionally rotate them. The child who finds a shiny blue rattle fascinating at five months of age will ignore it at ten months of age. Local libraries carry books that describe the types of toys or activities your baby is likely to be interested in at each stage of development.

Knowing what is an appropriate toy can best be determined by understanding what is not a toy. Tools, instruments, mechanical devices, or Mommy's and Daddy's private and personal property are not toys. Mommy's purse and the earrings, billfold, and lipstick in her purse are not toys. Neither is Dad's pocket pen or his hammer. Common sense and age consideration is a sufficient combination to guide any parent to age-appropriate toys.

If you have twins, alternate their times. Put one child in the playpen in the morning and the other in it in the afternoon. Occasionally try putting them both in at the same time.

If your home allows for it, vary the location of the playpen from time to time. For example, during the week you might put it in the living room. On the weekend place it near the sliding glass door overlooking the backyard where his siblings are playing. In warm weather, take the playpen outside. You should position the playpen so you can easily check on your child, but put it so your child cannot see you. It detracts from the purpose of self-focusing playtime if the child can see Mom or Dad. The choice between creative self-play or Mom sitting in the next room is not a fair choice to give a child. If you live in a small apartment, become creative. Use a portable room divider to section off part of the living room or bedroom.

The time your baby spends in the playpen will vary with age. During the first few months, your baby should have ten to twenty minutes twice a day in his playpen. By the time your baby can sit by himself, you can extend playpen time to fifteen to thirty minutes twice a day. Once your baby starts to crawl, increase the time to thirty to forty-five minutes at least once a day. Between fifteen and twenty months he can play up to one hour either in his playpen or possibly in his room. These are suggested times. Some days your child will play for longer periods, other days for less time.

Here we offer words of caution and encouragement. Do not overuse the playpen by leaving your baby in it for extended and unplanned periods during the day. Playpen time normally should be a planned activity, but not an all-day event. As a word of encouragement, children of all ages have a love/hate relationship with boundaries. They hate boundaries simply because they are there, yet love them because of the security they provide. That is true with the playpen. If your child does not appear to like it at first, stay with it, and later he will end up loving the playpen.

Starting Late

How would you introduce the playpen if it has not been part of your baby's day? Start with short increments of time——ten minutes a day. Over the next two weeks, work up to twenty-five minutes. After a month try thirty to forty-five minutes. There may be some crying, but the advantages gained outweigh the passing tears. With your next child, don't wait so long.

Roomtime

Between eighteen and twenty-two months of age, you can move your baby to *roomtime*. The principles of roomtime are the same as for the playpen, but you use his room as his play area. Parents should structure and plan this time into his day. Because he is in his room does not mean he can do as he pleases. He should not be allowed to ransack the room, take out all his toys, or rearrange the furniture. Some supervision is necessary. Initially, a gate may be required, but your goal is to have him play in his room by himself for an extended period of time without any physical restrictions. As he develops self-control and demonstrates responsible behavior, you can award him freedoms.

Many parents confuse roomtime with free playtime. Roomtime is assigned to the child. It's a time determined by Mom, not the child. Mothers will say to us, "My child plays in his room on his own." That's nice, but will he play in his room when Mom says to? Usually the answer is no. Just because a child voluntarily plays in his room does not mean he is having roomtime. It's one thing for a child to do what he wants when he wants to; it's another thing for him to do what is instructed.

Yielding to parental instruction as the normative of behavior is part of the learning structure you're attempting to establish. The self-control inherent in obedience is the same self-control that advances the child in other disciplines.

Time with Family Members

There are some obvious activities that take place during waketime that include interaction with one or more family members. It is important to enjoy your relationship with your pretoddler, but you must find the right balance between playing with your child and becoming your child's sole source of entertainment.

There is no right amount of time that must be devoted toward family play activities. But if you find that your child clings to you, refuses to go to Dad or siblings, and cries when you leave the room, it may be the result of too much playtime with Mom. In this case, the child is overly dependent on Mom for entertainment. He is comfortable only with her and thus closes off opportunities for others to participate in his life. Here are some safe play activities in which all family members can participate.

1. *Reading:* It is never too soon to read to your baby or

to show him colorful picture books (especially cardboard or plastic ones that the baby can explore on his own). Many children enjoy being read to long before they can understand the words. The continuous flow of sound and the changes in vocal inflections and facial expressions attract a child's attention. Nestling your child in your lap when you read further enhances this experience.

2. *Bathing*: This is another activity of your baby's day when interaction takes place. You can sing to him, tell him which part of his body you are washing, or just have fun splashing. However, you should ensure that splashing does not get out of hand. Remember that balance is the key concept in the training process. We recommend you bathe your baby and not bathe with him. A child may have several bath props such as plastic toys, a cup, or a spoon that make bathing a fun time.

3. *Walking:* Taking time for a stroll outside is a great activity for the two of you. By six months of age, your baby becomes fascinated with the treasure of God's creations. A regular walk becomes a big adventure for your pretoddler, and it is healthy for you.

4. *Touching*: A healthy influence on a child's emotional development is the type of physical touching that comes through play activities. Play is an important part of a child's growth. Touch communicates intimacy, and together touch and play form a winning combination. Lying down on the couch, floor, or bed and blowing kisses, tickling, and physically playing

with your baby are necessary components in healthy relationship formation.

Free Playtime

Free playtime does not mean you allow your baby to cruise the house looking to entertain himself. Rather, it refers to planned and impromptu times when a baby plays with his toys at a *play center*. A play center is a small, safe area containing a basket or box of age-appropriate toys that he can go to at will. Parents can set up play centers in the kitchen, bedroom, living room, or any convenient spot that will allow them to observe the child from a distance. Keep the majority of toys at the play center. That does not mean that if the play center is in the kitchen there would be no toys in his bedroom. But it does mean that toys are not left in every corner of the house for the child's convenience.

Play is important to a child. The repetition of play activities gives a child the chance to consolidate the skills the play objects require. It also affords him the opportunity to resolve mechanical problems with his play objects. For example, a child first finds the drawer open on the toy cash register. He shuts it but cannot figure out how to open it again. Here trial-and-error learning plays its part. Through finger manipulation and investigation, eventually the child learns the right keys to push to open the drawer. The child will use these problem-solving techniques in the toddler stage of development if afforded sufficient and controlled opportunities in the pretoddler stage.

Another parent-directed skill is clean-up. When play is over, help your child with this task without trying to do it all for him. Say to your child, "Playtime is over, let's clean up. Mommy will help," or, "Let's put your toys in your play box." By directing him to put some, if not all, of the toys back, you are defining the parameters of playtime. Those parameters include the concept that playtime is not over until all the toys are picked up. That process instills a sense of orderliness. It also impresses on the child a sense of personal responsibility.

In the pretoddler and early toddler months, keep the toys simple. Stacking blocks, balls, hand-manipulating objects, and colorful books are but a few examples. Play is important, and free playtime is as important as structured playpen time and roomtime. Enjoy your child and let him enjoy exploring the world through play.

SUMMARY

The type of behavioral adjustments a child makes in life is greatly influenced by his understanding of his environment, other people, and his growing awareness of self. Waketime serves growth and development. But waketime activities must be organized, and not free-for-all experiences falling between meals and naps. When a child receives guidance in establishing right patterns of behavior, learning is advanced.

QUESTIONS FOR REVIEW

1. What does the establishment of right learning patterns ultimately affect?
    Future intellectual development

2. What is learning deprivation? When does it occur?

Learning deprivation occurs when learning is left only to chance rather than maximizing all opportunities.

3. What is meant by the statement: "Learning opportunities should be predominantly the result of planning——not chance"?

Learning should be planned to help child learn to focus, self-control.

4. What is the difference between roomtime and free play-time?

Roomtime is time when older toddler 18-24 M plays on their own in a structured environment.

Free playtime is when kid is playing at a play center. (Corner where toys are kept). Child may explore toys + play

[81]

5. What is a play center?

Playcenter is a corner of the room where toys are kept.

6. Why is play important to a child?

Helps them learn skills.

Chapter Six
A Word About Discipline

Moral learning comes as a result of moral discipline. Discipline is a process of training and learning that fosters self-control and moral development. It comes from the same word *disciple*——one who is a learner. Discipline is a positive word, not a punitive action.

Children are not endowed at birth with self-control, nor is your pretoddler or toddler experienced enough in life to know how to morally discipline himself. Parents fulfill that role as teachers, while children are disciples who learn from them a way of life. Parents are the moral conscience of their children and are to act on their children's behalf until they reach moral maturity.

When we refer to child discipline, we are implying one thought: training——moral training. Moral training helps the child gain personal self-control. Self-control in turn helps the child with controlling his tongue and his actions, handling negative emotions, and making sound judgments. Proper discipline will guide a child to a life of integrity. It will help him be nonoffensive, filled with caring deeds. Most importantly, the positive effects of moral discipline are seen in the results: Content children who have the confidence to know why right is right and wrong is wrong and the self-control to consistently make the right decisions. The reason we discipline our children is to prepare them to face any circumstance of life wisely.

CORRECTIVE DISCIPLINE AND EARLY TRAINING

The foundations of moral training begin early and begin with basic discipline. Getting your baby on a routine and able to sleep through the night, are the results of basic discipline. As your child grows, so grows his need for moral guidance, encouragement, and correction.

Since the principle function of discipline is to teach morally responsible behavior, parents should educate, guide, and emphasize inner growth, personal responsibility, and self-control. These qualities lead to behavior motivated from the heart of the child. We educate our children by teaching them what is expected. We guide them by encouraging right behavior, and discouraging wrong behavior. From those two activities inner growth and self-control are established.

Many parents consider discipline to be a means of controlling the child's actions for the moment. That is true, but only partially so. The primary objective of early discipline is to lay down a foundation on which the next stage of development is built. Young children learn from concrete experience, not abstract parental reasoning. Train by instruction and reinforce compliance with encouragement and correction. Initially you will encourage and correct your child's actions. In time, your focus will be his heart from where his actions originate.

Training the Heart

For some theorists, parenting is a matter of facilitating a child's natural and impulsive way rather than actively directing the child's moral conscience. Reactive in nature, their nondirective approach seeks to control a child's environment in hopes of making it psychologically safe. Therefore, their theory forces the conclusion that comprehensive moral training that requires moral conformity is adversarial. It is adversarial, and it is supposed to be. If there is no conflict stimulating growth, then there is no thinking person at the other end of your correction. Permissive parenting dehumanizes children by taking away the conflict that prepares them for moral independence. They become robotic, controlled by passions and impulses but not moral thought.

BABYWISE II discipline is not the opposite, for the opposite is extreme——overindulgent, manipulative, and often unrealistic in its demands. Healthy discipline is positively different. The primary consideration is the child's heart and intrinsic motivation, not extrinsic manipulation.

There is something about the human heart that requires a parent's attention. And what is in the heart of a child? The old proverb "foolishness is bound up in the heart of a child" is an accurate anthropologic description. That means a child is born with the propensity to defy parental leadership and foolishly tries to guide himself. Foolishness in the heart means a child is attempting to act wise without the benefit of wisdom. The job of the parent is to transform the heart from what it is to what it should be. Everything is geared toward one common goal: taking the foolishness that is naturally part of a child and replacing it with wisdom.

Childishness and Foolishness

Throughout the training process and especially when your child moves into the toddler phase of growth, you will do well to understand the distinction between the words *foolishness* and *childishness*. Foolishness is any conscious act of willful defiance. You say, "Don't touch!" but he touches anyway. That is foolishness. In contrast, childishness is associated with innocent immaturity——the honest mistakes children make.

Parents, please understand that a child is not acting childish if he is disobedient——he is acting foolish. And he is not acting foolish when he makes innocent mistakes——he is acting childish. Both are in need of correction but the method of correction is different because the motive of the heart is different. One is malicious defiance, one is not. Understanding these distinctions will be of great assistance to you throughout your parenting years.

Foolishness needs correction, but parents should not correct all foolish behavior the same way, or with the same consequence. When correcting your pretoddler, toddler, and young child, there are four factors to consider:

1. the commonness of the particular offense
2. the context of the moment
3. the child's age, and
4. the general characterization of his overall behavior.

Always consider these four factors when making a judicial decision concerning your child's behavior. As you do, you will avoid exasperating your child, and yet at the same time, provide the corrective guidance needed.

ESSENTIALS OF DISCIPLINE

Since healthy discipline tries to develop *internal* management by educating the child in moral principle, there will be times when controlled force is necessary to bring about the desired goal. Here we offer this warning: controlled force without moral guidance is authoritarian; guidance without sufficient controls is permissive.

There will be many times when your child will reject or strongly oppose your reasonable instructions. What should you do? Teach the child to obey according to the character of true obedience——immediately, completely, without challenge, and without complaint. That task is not as difficult as it may seem. True obedience is often more difficult for the parent than for the child, for children only respond to parental resolve and nothing more.

Judicial parenting does not allow defiant behavior to be rewarded by doing nothing about it. For small faults, wisdom may dictate that you demonstrate patience or give a stern warning. But you should not consider direct and willful defiance trivial. Obedience and disobedience are moral acts, not individual preferences.

By obedience, we do not refer to the yielding that results from repeated threats, bribes, or manipulation of a child through the fear of losing parental love. Far worse than these methods is that of adult persuasion. You cannot govern a child by mere logic and argument. He does not possess your moral mind; he is not your moral peer. To reason with a one-year-old child in hopes of bringing him into moral conformity is like reasoning with the wind. Better to lead, direct, and guide with your rightful authority instead of craftiness. You are the parent, you know best. For the sake of your child, insist on his compliance.

Principles of Instruction

All training begins with parental instruction. When we consider the role of instruction in a child's life, there are a few facts and elementary principles that serve as a guide to success for all of your parenting years. Following these basic guidelines can prevent stress and increase willful compliance; failure to comply can lead to power struggles and continuous outright rebellion as your child moves into toddlerhood.

Principle One

When you speak to your child in a way that requires an answer or an action, you should expect a response. Children will rise to the level of expectation of their parents. Too many parents expect little and receive exactly that. We find consistently that the requirement of first-time obedience is far less of an adjustment for children than it is for their parents.

Principle Two

Never give a command unless you intend for it to be obeyed. Therefore, when giving instructions be sure to say exactly what you mean and mean precisely what you say. This simple principle is so commonly violated. There is no better way to teach a child not to obey than to give him instructions that you have no intention of enforcing. A child quickly learns the habit of disregarding a parents' instruction if there is no resolve behind it. Children by nature are gamblers. The absence of clear instruction encourages them to gamble that you will do nothing.

Principle Three

Healthy discipline is always consistent. The child who is corrected consistently for failing to obey is better adjusted than the child whose discipline is inconsistent or incomplete. Consistency provides security and freedom. The child knows what is expected and what is off-limits.

In contrast, inconsistency produces insecurity, and because the boundaries are always in question, it stifles a child's learning and his learning potential. Consistent discipline helps the child to learn that there is a moral orderliness in the world; certain behaviors will always be followed by disappointing consequences or punishment and other behaviors will be followed by praise and encouragement.

Be consistent with your discipline! Consistency keeps you at the right point at each stage of development. Inconsistency creates too many variables for the child to handle, forcing you to do more parenting outside the funnel. When parents reduce or eliminate variables that are not age-appropriate from their child's environment, they establish right learning patterns more quickly and firmly. Order facilitates healthy growth, unlike excessive freedom, which leads to developmental confusion.

Encouraging and establishing right moral behavior in children requires consistency and clarity of instruction. Wholesome discipline is always consistent. Unless your instructions are clear and consistent, your child is at a loss to know what to do.

Principle Four

Require eye contact when giving face-to-face instruction.

Make it a standard practice to get your child to look you in the eyes when you are speaking. Eye contact is a focusing skill and helps any child process instructions. The child that is allowed to look around rather than at Mom or Dad as instructions are given often struggles with compliance.

Principle Five

Understanding context prevents first-time obedience from becoming legalistic. Unless you give due consideration to the context of the moment, you may judge your child's right actions wrongly, and you may neglect wrong actions entirely.

Reinforcing Parental Instruction

As your child becomes more mobile, he naturally will explore his growing world. Help him assimilate to his expanding world gradually. Parents should neither prevent exploration nor grant absolute freedom. There is a healthy balance between those two extremes. Releasing your child to freedom must be in accordance with the responsible behavior required by those freedoms.

The living room, for example, is only off-limits to the child who does not have self-control over his hands. After the child has learned what he can and cannot touch, combined with the exercise of self-restraint, parents may allow the child access to the rest of the living room.

The plant resting on the fireplace hearth was off-limits to eight-month-old Whitney. Two attempts, two no's, and two swats to her hand established Whitney's understanding that most of the living room is touchable, but not the plant. She learned, retained, and imposed self-restrictions. The developmental significance of that training was that the future freedom granted her far outweighed her momentary cry of disappointment. Do not fear the use of restraint or the light to moderate swat to the hand. You are not teaching your child violence, to hit other children, or that power comes in strength. But you are teaching him concretely the current limits of life.

People commonly wonder what an eight or nine month old really can understand and how long they can remember. It is amazing what a trained pretoddler mind can comprehend and retain. For example, Grandpa was sitting on the couch when he showed Ashley a cookie. He hid the cookie just under the cushion then invited her to find it. She immediately went to the cushion and took the cookie. Two weeks later, she visited again. Once in the house she went right to the cushion and looked for another cookie. She was clearly disappointed to find nothing, but everyone realized that her memory worked just fine. Although memory retention is enhanced by pleasure, parents should keep in mind that it is also reinforced by displeasure——the type that comes when parents set needed boundaries.

Directive and Restrictive Instruction

Paralleling a child's increased mobility is his cognitive aptitude for understanding basic instructions. Not only does he understand, but he is capable of learning how to appropriately respond.

Parental instruction is either *directive* (telling a child what to do) or *restrictive* (telling a child what not to do). Both categories require a response of immediate compliance and are achievable because of the child's ability to understand. Do not underestimate how early that skill is developed.

Directive Instructions

Directive instructions require a response. That response is trainable. Parents can start calling attention to a right response as soon as their baby begins to show signs of mobility. For example, as soon as your baby begins to crawl, call him and then walk to where he is, pick him up, take him to where you want him to go, and then verbally encourage him by saying, "Good, you're learning to obey Mama." This helps your child become accustomed to your command voice and your praise voice that accompanies the right response.

As your child becomes more mobile, and you sense he grasps the concept of coming, then require conformity. That will be achieved by the combination of such words of encouragement as, "Good boy Ryan, you're obeying Mama," or applying one of the four age-appropriate corrections.

Restrictive Instructions

Yes, a nine-month-old *BABYWISE* baby really can understand basic restrictive instructions. Simple commands such as "stop," "no," "do not touch," or "do not move" are usually the first restrictive commands of early parenting. To bring meaning to those words, "stop" must mean stop, "no" must mean no, "do not touch," must mean do not touch, and "do not move" must mean do not move. These are four different commands with a common link——the requirement of first-time obedience. The sooner parents instill the reality of first-time obedience within the child, the fewer behavioral problems they will observe and the more freedoms the child will enjoy. Obedience is important. You should establish it early for your child's benefit.

There will be times when your child will ignore or strongly oppose your instructions. When that happens, what will you do? In Chapter Four, we introduced the four age-appropriate options for reinforcing parental instructions. Those options included verbal reprimands, isolation, loss of privilege (or toy), and swatting the hand. As your child increases his skills of motoring around the house, those options must be activated if you hope to gain control over your child's impulsive behavior. Children will only respond to parental resolve. What is your resolve?

SETTING BOUNDARIES

To set a boundary means to limit (but not abolish) a child's freedom of: movement, environment, choices, and speech. For health, safety, and moral reasons, setting boundaries denies a child access to something he wants or wants to do. It could be the on/off button on the stereo, the hair on your dog's back, the glasses on Dad's nose, or the pen in your pocket.

The purpose of limiting your child is not to curtail his freedom of exploration but to give him freedom within manageable limits, according to his timetable of understanding. A child possessing more freedom than he can handle or more right of access that he can manage will get himself in trouble. This speaks to one of the many paradoxes in development. A child cannot enjoy freedom without surrendering some of it.

Some parents are afraid to say "no" or "don't touch" to their pretoddler. "No" is not a bad word for you to avoid at all costs. For a pretoddler and toddler, it simply defines the necessary boundaries. The word *no* is the furthest extreme of the word *yes*. Most of your home is an unspoken yes, but there are some items that for now must remain off-limits to his little hands.

The key to setting limits for your mobile pretoddler is not in controlling his environment (although that will be done) but in instilling a right response to your instructions. The goal is to train him to your voice (which includes tone and modulation), not to the object. Your voice and tone are the constant factors of correction; the various objects in the living room are the variables.

When your child reaches out to touch an item off-limits to his little hands, instruct with a firm "no" or "that's a no." (Whatever statement you use, use it consistently.) If the child persists, then add a meaningful swat to his hand, (and hand only), while verbally repeating, "No, you need to obey Mama." If he pursues it again you have several options available. One is to repeat the swat. Swats need to count. Some reasonable discomfort is necessary. The mother that says, "I swat his hand but he just smiles at me" obviously is not swatting hard enough to bring some mild discomfort.

If you apply the appropriate amount of discomfort and the child still returns to the object in defiance, then you should isolate him to a toy-free crib. The time spent in isolation will vary based on the age of the child, the time of day, and the nature of the offense. Periods of isolation may be as short as five minutes. That will be time enough to get your point across.

Will your child begin to associate his crib with a place

of punishment? Will that affect his naps or nighttime sleep? To both questions, the answer is No! Your pre-toddler is able to discriminate between times of isolation and bedtimes. The factors surrounding isolation are contrary to those surrounding bedtime. The hugs and kisses associated with sleeptime are noticeably absent in correction. Parental behavior is what cues the child as to what is going on, not the crib itself.

A third option is to remove the child (not the object) from the irresistible source of temptation. You might transport the child to his play center, saying, "Play here. These are Ryan's toys."

Power Struggles

Can a nine month old pull a parent into a power struggle? Yes. Many do it everyday! A power struggle results when parents fail to exercise their authority wisely. That is, they allow themselves to be forced into a "must-win" situation over a seemingly minor conflict. There will be some early parent-child conflicts in which parental resolve must be victorious, but you should choose well which hill you're willing to die on. Wise parenting is superior to power parenting.

Here is an example of how a minor comflict can turn into a serious battle of the wills. The gas heater was off-limits to Ryan's little hands. When he touched it, he received a verbal reprimand from Mom and a swat to his hand. Undeterred, he began to play with it again, once more he heard the word *no*, and received a second swat. He touched it a third time, and then a fourth. Back and forth they went. Ryan's mom is now in a full-blown power struggle. If she gives up, Ryan learns that persistence pays off and obedience is optional. If she continues swatting him, she moves perilously close to abuse.

This is a common pretoddler scenario. There is a way to defuse the potential power struggle and maintain the integrity of your authority. Using the example above, the mom after the second swat should have isolated Ryan to his crib or bodily removed him to another room. In either case, she would have wisely exercised her parental authority and defused the power struggle. Such actions would achieve her goal without compromise to her authority and without manipulating the environment.

Surrendering with Dignity

A ten month old should be allowed the freedom to surrender with dignity. Let's return to Ryan and the gas heater to demonstrate this concept. A child will often defy a parent when the parent makes the option of surrender intolerable. That is, a child will persist with wrong behavior if a parent does not give him room to surrender with dignity.

When Ryan's mom battled him toe-to-toe, her very presence made surrendering to her authority difficult if not impossible. If she had walked away from him after her second swat and verbal reprimand, he most likely would have left the gas heater alone. Mom's presence extended the conflict. By leaving, she gave him some room to surrender with dignity rather than face a continued challenge. If she had to go back a third time, then removing Ryan would have been the best option. That is wisdom parenting, not power parenting. The dignity of your child, even in correction must be preserved. Do it graciously.

Babyproofing the House

Restricting a child's freedom in the major rooms of your house is called "babyproofing." That term has legitimate and illegitimate meanings. The first refers to making your home safe for your crawler and early walker. Parents need to be concerned with important safety issues. Do you have a tipsy bookcase? If so, secure it to the wall. Do you have electrical outlets overloaded with extension cords? Move them. Make your baby's learning environment safe.

The illegitimate side of babyproofing deals with rearranging the entire living room so that the child is never put into a position where restrictions apply. With the exclusion of removing dangerous or priceless items, there is no need to rearrange your home; however, there is a need to train your child regarding what is appropriate and what is off-limits to his little hands. When the child starts touching the off-limit items, you should apply the appropriate consequences.

In general, parents who place no demands on their children have children that will take advantage of parental uncertainty and assert themselves motivated by impulsive behavior and not moral thought. When their acts become intolerable, and their parents attempt to suppress the rebellion, the children develop feelings of contempt for the parents' "softness." Future behavioral problems that result from the lack of boundary setting are usually more serious than those engendered by overly strict discipline.

As a word of encouragement, parents who raise their children by the principles of *BABYWISE* find that they have a much greater propensity to yield themselves to parental instruction during this stage of development than children who are demand-fed. A child raised with immediate self-gratification early in life is less prepared to handle the conflict that boundaries create later on——usually the parents are too.

SUMMARY

Healthy discipline consists of a number of essential principles and actions, some encouraging, some corrective. The encouraging side for the pretoddler includes affirmation, praise, and rewards. The corrective side consists of verbal reproof, natural consequences, isolation, restrictions, loss of privileges, and swatting of the hand. Each activity has purpose, meaning, and a legitimate place in the overall process.

QUESTIONS FOR REVIEW

1. What is the primary consideration of discipline?

    - la process that fosters self-control + moral training
    - Comes from the word disciple or one who learns

2. What is the definition of the word *foolishness*? What is *childishness*?

    - foolishness is a child who touches a hot stove after being told not to
    - childishness are mistakes that kids make

3. Summarize the five principles of instruction.

a. When you speak to your kid expect a response.

b. Never give a command unless you find for it to be obeyed.

c. Healthy discipline is always consistent

d. Eye contract is required during instruction.

e. Understand the context of the situation.

4. The four restrictive commands of early parenting are "stop," "no," "do not touch," and "do not move." To bring complete meaning to those words, what must happen?

There must be 1st time obedience,

5. In reference to boundary setting, what does the word *no* represent?

No simply defines the boundaries

Chapter Seven
Nap and Sleeptime Activities

As stated in *BABYWISE*, where there is ability, there is also a natural capacity. Your baby has already demonstrated both the natural ability and capacity to sleep through the night. It was an acquired skill resulting from right training. This chapter focuses on sleep-related activities for both your pretoddler and toddler. We conclude our discussion by responding to a number of common sleep-related questions.

NAPS AND NIGHTTIME SLEEP

Unlike feeding patterns, infant sleep behavior has more variation because of individual differences. Remember, stable sleep patterns are based on stable hunger patterns. When there are a number of disruptions in your baby's eating patterns, there will be corresponding changes in his sleep patterns. If there are a number of disruptions with his evening sleep (e.g., as when traveling), his daytime behavior can be greatly affected.

Sleep is an important part of a baby's life and will

continue to be a great part of your pretoddler's day and night. Children in the pretoddler phase will not differ considerably in the amount of time they spend sleeping. That may change in the toddler phase, but for now continue encouraging healthy patterns of sleep.

Naptime

Naps are not an option based on your baby's wants. When naptime comes, the baby goes down. It is that simple. For optimal development, children need daytime rest. A toddler's ability to take a nap depends on the habits he has developed in his first year. Do not underestimate the importance of your baby's nap. Naps will tend to fall in place naturally. Even when your routine changes and your baby is more wakeful, naps are still very important.

At six months of age, the average *BABYWISE* baby takes two 1 1/2- to 2-hour naps and an additional "catnap" in the late afternoon. By eight months of age, he will require only the morning and afternoon naptimes. That pattern continues until the child reaches approximately 18-20 months. Around that age, the morning nap is dropped, leaving only the afternoon nap.

Waking up Happy

A parent's belief about sleep highly influences a baby's wake-up disposition. Your baby's wake-up disposition can be happy and content when you follow three basic rules.

Rule One: Mom, not the baby, decides when the nap starts.

Rule Two: Mom, not the baby, decides when the nap ends.

Rule Three: If your baby wakes up crying or cranky, it is most often because he has not had sufficient sleep. He may have awakened due to a dirty diaper, a noisy neighbor, the beginning of sickness, or an arm or leg stuck between the crib slats.

If you leave him in his crib, even though he may fuss or cry, he will probably go right back to sleep (in ten minutes or less) for another rest period extending thirty to forty minutes.

When your baby gets enough sleep, you will notice a happy disposition. The baby will make cooing sounds, letting you know it is time to get him up. Balance is important. There will be times when your pretoddler and toddler may need five minutes of comfort in Mom's or Dad's arms as he adjusts from naptime to waketime. Those moments can be some of the most precious of all in your parenting.

Nighttime Sleep

At six months of age, your baby's nighttime sleep patterns are well established, and an average of ten to twelve hours of continuous sleep is the norm. Those patterns will change little over the next eighteen months, with a few brief exceptions due to illness.

COMMON SLEEP PROBLEMS

As we use the word "common," we do so in reference to

BABYWISE babies and not babies in general. The common problems for a demand-fed baby are not experienced by babies on a routine. As you discovered with the success of *BABYWISE*, sleep problems for your baby have much less to do with *nature* than with *nurture*.

Sleep is a natural function of the body. The primary cue for infant sleep is sleepiness. Sleep cues are influenced (often negatively) by a variety of sleep association props. Some sleep props, such as a special blanket or stuffed animal, are usually harmless, while others, such as the nighttime bottle, pacifier, and thumbsucking, can be addictive. The problem with sleep props is not getting the child to fall asleep initially, but helping him learn to get back to sleep without the prop.

The Nighttime Bottle

For the older baby, the most common sleep prop is the nighttime bottle. Too many children become conditioned to going to bed with a bottle and depend on it to fall asleep. You can avoid the bottle prop by not getting in the habit of putting him down with one. That does not mean he will never take a bottle in his crib. There will be some naptimes when baby, bottle, and crib form a convenient alliance for a busy mom. As long as this behavior does not become habit forming, it will not become addictive.

Rotate the Blankets

So that your child does not become overly attached to one blanket, consider limiting its use to the crib/bed or occasionally on long car rides. Do not let your pretoddler drag it everywhere he goes. Although a common blanket provides a sense of familiarity, true security is tied to relationships, not objects.

Pacifier

There are many good reasons for using a pacifier with your newborn. But by six months of age, any need for additional nonnutritive sucking is greatly diminished. Does your child need a pacifier to fall asleep? If so, now is the time to start breaking the habit.

Experience and common sense teach that it is easier to do away with the pacifier at six months than at twelve or eighteen months of age. At six months, parents can just take it away. Yes, there probably will be some crying, but no emotional damage. If your child is older, you can prepare him a few days in advance with some encouraging words and finally a gentle "no more." Another suggestion is to pierce the pacifier with a needle and release the vacuum. The vacuum bubble is what makes the pacifier enjoyable; when that is gone, the pleasure is gone, often resulting in the child weaning himself.

Thumb Sucking

Of the two nonnutritive sucking techniques, thumb sucking is the most difficult to control. We can take away the pacifier but not the child's fingers. As with many adult habits, parents will not be able to break the habit of thumb sucking overnight. It is a gradual process that requires consistency on the part of the parents. The way you break the nighttime habit is to break the daytime habit.

If your child is between six and eighteen months of age, limit his thumb sucking to naps and bedtime only. When you see his thumb in the mouth, gently pull it out, say, "Not now," and redirect the child to appropriate play.

Teething and General Sickness

Teething can disrupt nighttime sleep. When a tooth begins to break through the gum, you have the condition commonly referred to as teething. Like jaundice, teething is not a disease, but a condition of growth. Your baby's first teeth will push through between six and eight months of age. By six months, one baby out of three has one tooth; by nine months, the average baby has three teeth. Teething should not interfere with breast-feeding, since the sucking is done by the tongue and palate, not by the gums.

Discomfort, irritability, fussiness, increased salivation, and a slightly raised temperature can accompany the eruption of a tooth. As uncomfortable as a child might appear, parents should not regard teething as a catch-all excuse for chronic poor behavior or a drastic change in their baby's routine.

Obviously teething can disrupt nighttime sleep. How can you comfort your baby and at the same time avoid establishing poor sleep habits? First, understand that the process of cutting teeth does not disrupt sleep in all babies (especially PDF babies). There is still discomfort but not enough to override the well-established sleep patterns. Second, understand the temporary nature of the condition. Babies do not cut teeth for weeks. The norm is usually a couple of days. Your local pharmacy has over-the-counter teething gels that serve to numb the gums.

Usually the numbing is limited so acetaminophen is commonly recommended to help the baby relax and go to sleep.

If the problem is so serious that it keeps your baby awake, comfort him by rocking, but do not take him in bed with you or feed him. Sleeping with you will not make the child's gums feel better, but it will promote an undesirable sleep prop. Comfort when comfort is needed, but when those teeth finally break through, get back to your regular routine. If your child continues to wake during the night, it is not from need but habit. He must relearn how to fall back to sleep on his own. That will not take long at all.

You can handle illnesses in a similar fashion. Stay as close to your routine as possible and follow your doctor's advice regarding the use of medication. Usually a decrease in appetite will accompany an illness. Do not force your child to eat but maintain adequate liquid intake as prescribed by your pediatrician.

Provide comfort when comfort is needed but avoid habit-forming practices that will only need correction in the future. After an illness passes, it may take up to three days before your child accepts the reality of his old routine. So, once your child returns to health, get back to your routine.

MOVING FROM A CRIB TO A BED

Moving a child from a crib to a bed takes place in the toddler phase of development, not the pretoddler phase. The crib-to-bed transition usually occurs between eighteen and twenty-four months of age. A child who is trained to first-time obedience greatly facilitates this transition. It should be obvious that if parents do not require first-time obedience during the day, then instructions to stay in bed at night or during naps will have no power. Going from a crib to a bed is a freedom. What will keep him there? Only your word. The goal is not to only put your child in a bed but to have him stay there all night.

To help make the transition smooth for you and exciting for your child, include him when going out to purchase his bed. Maybe he could help Dad set it up, or shop with Mom to pick out his "big boy" sheets for his "big boy" bed. Take advantage of the weekend to make the switch. Most dads will be home Saturday morning to make a big deal out of a child's first night in his own bed.

Initially, do not give your child the freedom to get out of bed without your permission. After his naps or in the morning, have him call out to you before getting out of bed. Teach him a common phrase such as "Up please" or "May I get up please?" Letting him have verbal access to you is usually enough to keep him in bed.

Finally, when making the transition, buy or build a side rail. Children move during their sleep much more than adults. Side rails are as much for the parents' peace of mind as for the child's safety.

QUESTIONS ABOUT PRETODDLER SLEEP

Having surveyed many *BABYWISE* mothers and fathers, the following represent the most commonly asked questions regarding pretoddler sleep.

1. Our six month old has always slept through the night. Now all of a sudden he is waking and crying. Why is this happening? What should we do?

This is not an uncommon problem and can occur anytime between five and eight months. There are four common reasons why babies wake at night. The *first reason* is hunger. His waking may be a signal that he is ready for solids. The *second reason* is associated with the third nap (late afternoon). It may be time to drop the full nap and move to a catnap or no nap at all. With three full naps a day, the baby is now getting too much sleep. The *third reason* for waking at night is teething. It is easier to identify this since daytime irritability accompanies the condition. The *fourth reason* for nighttime waking is associated with changes in your baby's daytime routine. Has there been a major change in it? Has this been a busy week? Do you have relatives visiting who feel it is their responsibility to hold your baby all day? Are you just getting back from a trip? Check your baby's routine.

2. Our six-month-old baby is sleeping fine at night but all of a sudden is waking forty-five minutes into each nap. Is this normal? Should we get him up?

It is not uncommon for PDF pretoddlers between five and eight months of age to begin waking halfway through their naps and give all the appearance of being ready to get up. If this begins to happen with your baby, do not get him up. Instead, train him to fall back to sleep on his own. Pretoddlers need to nap longer than forty-five minutes.

This new wake phenomenon can last anywhere from three days to three weeks. The root cause appears to be associated with a new sense of alertness that accompanies the pretoddler phase of development. In *BABYWISE*, we discussed the rotating relaxed sleep patterns (RSP) and the active sleep patterns (ASP). As your child comes out of his first relaxed sleep state, his new sense of alertness is affected by familiar sounds. It could be the sound of a door shutting, the furnace going on, the school bus outside bringing home siblings, or a host of other familiar noises. The alertness seems to trigger curiosity and instead of falling back to sleep, he wakes and calls for you.

Your child needs to learn how to fall back to sleep and not let his curiosity control his sleep patterns. Rather, allow his sleep patterns to control his untimely curiosity. You can check to make sure everything is okay, but ultimately you need to leave him in his crib to fall back to sleep.

Unfortunately, in order to correct this condition some crying will take place. The cry is not one of need but of desire. As you were taught in *BABYWISE*, do not respond to a baby's cry mindlessly but rationally consider what is best for the baby in the long run. In this case, the continuance of excellent sleep behavior is far more important than the emotional disturbance of your baby's cry.

3. Our child is now standing in his crib but doesn't know how to get back down and begins to cry. What should we do?

Standing in the crib is half of a newly acquired skill. The other half is learning how to sit down after standing. You can aid the process by taking a few minutes after each nap to show him how to sit down. Take his hands firmly and guide them down the crib slats helping him sit. Over time he will get use to the sensation of letting himself down. If you go in every time to put him down, then you're only delaying the learning process. There will be no need to learn to sit if he knows that when he cries you will always come in. This is another time when no response to a cry is the best response for the baby's sake.

4. Our child keeps losing his pacifier at night and begins to cry. What should we do?

As stated previously, a sleep prop is any device needed to help the child fall back to sleep once he awakens. In this case, the prop is the pacifier. The more you get up and return the pacifier to the child's mouth, the more you reinforce this wrong expectation. It's probably time to wean him from it.

5. Our baby throws off his covers at night, gets cold, and then begins to cry. What do we do?

Children move around in their sleep, making it difficult to stay covered. As parents, you only have three preventative options. Dress your child warmly at night, turn up your central heating, or purchase a safe room heater. One caution to consider concerning nighttime sleep and room heaters. Be careful not to place your baby too close to a heater in hopes of compensating for the coldness of the night. Overheating a child can be a greater health threat than being too cold.

6. My husband and I will be traveling for the next couple of weeks. How do we maintain the baby's routine,

especially when we move through other time zones?

There are two considerations to focus on when traveling: (1) *training your baby to sleep other places than in his crib,* and (2) *adjusting his routine to each new time zone.*

In preparation for travel, begin a few weeks in advance putting your child down for his naps or nighttime sleep in his playpen. For a couple of nights, put the playpen in the living room, family room, or your bedroom. Drape the outside of the playpen on two sides with towels or extra baby blankets, then bring those blankets or borrow some towels when on your trip. The towels serve to enclose the child's sleep environment and reduce potential distractions.

If your trip is within two time zones, time adjustments will be fairly automatic. When flying through three or four time zones, make the adjustments to your baby's routine once you arrive. The type of adjustment depends on whether you are traveling east to west or west to east. With the first, you have an extended day; with the second, you have an early night. If you have an extended day, add another feeding and possibly a catnap. If you go east, split the bedtime difference in half between the old and new time zones. For example, your baby's 7:00 p.m. West Coast bedtime is equivalent to 10:00 p.m. EST. Splitting the difference between the two time zones would make your baby's first East Coast bedtime 8:30 p.m. Over the next couple of days, work his bedtime back to 7:00 p.m., making as many adjustments as needed to his daytime routine.

We suggest you limit sweet drinks and snacks while traveling. A trip is not the time to add extra sugar to your baby's diet, and extra snacks can suppress hunger to the point where it can affect digestive stabilization. Disrupting your baby's hunger metabolism often affects the sleep/wake cycles. Overall, your PDF baby will be a joy to travel with, and what few problems you might encounter will be temporary.

7. My seven month old still fusses for five to ten minutes at each nap. Will he ever outgrow it?

Yes, he will. So do not change a thing you're doing. For some babies fussing is the only way to release pent-up emotional energy. As long as he is taking good naps, that little time of fussing will soon be a thing of the past.

SUMMARY

As your baby grows through the pretoddler and toddler phases, the amount of sleep needed will gradually decline, but the quality of sleep will remain. What problems you might encounter in your child's sleep behavior will be minor in comparison to the giant strides you made in sleep stabilization. Your proactive mindset for parenting and your common sense will help you meet any sleep challenges that might come up.

BABYWISE II has taken you to another level of understanding of the amazing world of your baby. You can take comfort in seeing the obvious——your child is now ahead in so many ways. Keep up the good work.

QUESTIONS FOR REVIEW

1. What are the three "wake-up happy" rules?

   a. Mom/Dad decides when the nap starts.

   b. Mom/Dad decides when nap ends.

   c. If Hannah wakes up crying or cranky, it's because of lack of sleep

2. By definition, what is the problem with sleep props?

   Sleep props get the little ones in the habit of not going to sleep unless the prop is there.

3. What is the one thing that will keep a child from getting out of bed?

   - Side rail

   - Knowing 1st time obedience

4. List four reasons why PDF babies begin waking up at night during the early pretoddler phase.

   a. Because they are hungry (Ready for solid food).

   b. Sleeping too Much during the day.

   c. teething

   d. Changes in the baby's routine during the day.

5. Why do some babies wake up early from their naps? What should you do about it?

   Babyies sometimes wake up early from their naps due to a new sense of alertness. You Should let them fuss + go back to sleep.

Appendix A
Child Language Development

Anyone attempting to learn a language can tell you that it can be a very difficult task, and it takes years to achieve any sort of fluency. Babies come equipped with a phenomenal ability to achieve total fluency in about three years, with very little practice and almost no conscious thought required. Parents are the models for a child's development, and the area of language development is no different from the many others discussed in this guide. Here are some ideas to help encourage your child's language development.

1. It is not necessary to use "baby talk." It is very tempting to reduce what you are saying to what you think the baby understands, such as "Ryan, no touch, that bad." Children are wonderful decoders. If you say, "Ryan, don't touch that, it's bad," he will (even at the young age of six months) understand the tone of voice, the facial expression, and any gestures you might use. By twelve to fourteen months, he'll understand enough of the words and intonations to figure out exactly what you are telling him. Children are wonderful imitators too. Why not give them a chance to learn the correct sentence structure?

2. Talk about anything and everything! This gives your child a chance to pair words with concepts. Even though he will not understand all the words at first, what a great exposure to the world you are giving him. When you go to the grocery store, talk about what you are getting, where you are going next, and things you see in the aisles. A pretoddler certainly

doesn't understand everything, but you are laying a broad foundation for the future.

3. Read, read, read! Reading books to your child is a wonderful way to expose him to words and concepts. (We recommend Jim Trelease's *Read-Aloud Handbook*, Penguin Books: N.Y., N.Y.)

4. Once your child starts speaking, expand on what he says. For example, you are giving your son a bath, and he says, "Boat down." You could respond by saying, "Yes, the boat went down." This not only recognizes what your child has said, but also gives him the correct form of a full sentence. Cute though it is, you really do not want your child to start kindergarten using baby sentences!

5. Above all, relax! With few exceptions, children learn language in spite of anything parents do or think they have done to inhibit it!

CHILD LANGUAGE DEVELOPMENT
The following is a general outline of the stages of child language development. Each child develops at his own rate, and the ages given are only approximate.

Birth to 3 months A familiar, friendly voice comforts him. He smiles at Mother or another familiar person. He has different cries for hunger, a dirty diaper, and fatigue. He coos and goos.

2 to 4 months He begins to pay attention to the per-

son speaking to him, responds to an angry tone of voice by crying, and turns toward a source of sound. He laughs out loud and begins to babble, making sounds like "bababa."

4 to 6 months   He begins to respond to his environment and begins to understand inflection and intensity of utterances. He strings several different sounds together ("badabadaba"), and he blows raspberries.

6 to 9 months   He listens with greater attention to other's utterances, and understands words such as no, bye-bye, and his name. He begins to echo sounds and actions that others make.

9 to 12 months   He begins following simple directions (do not touch, come here) and shakes his head yes and no. The long-awaited first word appears and he begins to "jargon" (strings of sounds paired with intonations to sound like questions, statements, demands).

12 to 18 months   He recognizes familiar objects and people and identifies body parts. He adds more and more words and begins to put short sentences together.

18 to 24 months   He identifies more and more objects

when requested to do so and listens to simple stories.

The ages listed above are only a guide, and indicate when most children exhibit the language skill listed. Don't worry if your child is a month or two late at attaining any given level; children mature at different rates. If your child is not speaking at all by the age of two years, or appears not to respond to you at all by the age of one year, you should seek referrals to the appropriate professionals from your child's doctor.

Appendix B
Teaching Your Child To Sign

To teach your child to sign is to teach him a second language. Like all skills, time, patience, and encouragement are required for success. Start with the basics (the first four listed) and then gradually expand his signing vocabulary. Have fun.

PLEASE
Rub chest with hand in a circular motion.

MORE
Bring the tips of fingers resting on thumbs. Bring tips of both hands together.

THANK YOU

Place tips of the hand (fingers together), against the mouth and throw it forward, similar to blowing a kiss.

ALL DONE

Hold both hands with fingers spread apart, palms facing chest. Shake palms away and down.

NO
Bring index and middle finger together to rest on thumb in one "snapping" motion.

I LOVE YOU
Extend and hold thumb, index, and little finger with palm facing toward subject.

MOMMY

With fingers spread apart, thumb touches middle of chin.

DADDY

With fingers spread apart, thumb touches middle of forehead.

EAT
All fingertips resting on thumb, bring hand toward mouth a couple of times.

THIRSTY
Bring tip of the index finger down throat.

HUNGRY

With hand in the shape of a C, place it just below it just below the throat, palm facing in, and bring it down.

DRINK

Place your hand in the shape of a C in front of mouth, thumb resting on chin, and bring hand up as if pouring a drink into mouth.

STOP
Little-finger side of the right hand is brought down quickly on the left palm. (As if you were cutting something in half.)

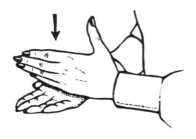

YES
With hand in a fist, "nod" it back and forth. (Similar to nodding your head.)

Appendix C
Hints On Potty Training

As a society, parents have gone from toilet training starting at one year to no real training at all. Both extremes are based on specific philosophies of life——behavioralism and neo-Freudianism. Like other areas of parenting, we know that a child does not have the ability to decide what is always best or to exhibit self-control. That is why parents with their superior wisdom are in control. Here are some commonsense suggestions to help you when the time for training arrives.

Signs of Readiness

1. Between eighteen and twenty-four months you may notice your toddler staying dry during naps or for two-hour periods, plus waking up either dry or nearly dry in the morning. This indicates that the bladder is able to hold urine for two or more hours.

2. Your toddler stops an activity while having a bowel movement or reports having had a bowel movement or wet diaper.

3. Your toddler expresses a desire to imitate parents or siblings using the toilet.

Once you see these signs on a regular basis, then:

1. Purchase a potty chair and have it in the bathroom so your toddler can become familiar with it.

2. As with other areas of parenting, develop a routine.

3. Place your toddler on the potty (tell the child; do not ask him if he would like to sit):

a. after each meal,
b. before going to bed and before naptime, and
c. when waking up in the morning and from naps.

Relax, be patient, and give your child a chance. Put your toddler in training pants for the naps and use diapers at night until you are confident of night dryness. Children vary in their ability to remain dry at night. You might begin right away by putting your child to bed in training pants and see how he does. The majority of children day and night train within a short period of time.

Since potty training is a skill, goal incentives can be used in the training process (M & M-type candy, raisins, or whatever is appropriate for your family). Many children become bladder trained before they accomplish bowel control. Once you know your child is capable of going but refuses, then you are facing a potential discipline issue. Like moving from the crib to a bed, what should keep your child on the potty is your voice command. As a general rule, parents who trained their children to first-time obedience have fewer problems in potty training than those parents who do not. If soiling continues to be a problem with a child over two and one-half years, hold him accountable for his own accidents. That means he must clean up himself and soiled clothes.

Once you start, stay with it. False starts are confusing and communicate to the child your own uncertainty. The older the child becomes, the more he realizes you have no control over this process, and it can become a discipline issue. Again, be patient and remember each child is unique, and the process takes time.

One final note: If your child is still on a bottle, not on any routine during the day, not sleeping through the night, naps inconsistently, sleeps with you, or does not obey instructions, then toilet training will not come easily. You must deal with those issues first.

Subject Index